To:

From:

365 Devotions to Inspire Your Day

hugs™

*Daily
Inspirations for
Moms*

HOWARD BOOKS
A DIVISION OF SIMON & SCHUSTER
New York   London   Toronto   Sydney

Our purpose at Howard Books is to:
• *Increase faith* in the hearts of growing Christians
• *Inspire holiness* in the lives of believers
• *Instill hope* in the hearts of struggling people everywhere

Because He's coming again!

Published by Howard Books, a division of Simon & Schuster, Inc.
1230 Avenue of the Americas, New York, NY 10020
www.howardpublishing.com

Hugs Daily Inspirations for Moms © 2007 Freeman-Smith, LLC

Library of Congress Cataloging-in-Publication Data
Hugs daily inspirations for moms / [compiled by Criswell Freeman].
    p. cm.
    1. Mothers—Prayer-books and devotions—English. I. Freeman, Criswell.
    BV4847.H84 2007
    242'.6431—dc22

                                                    2006049039

13 Digit ISBN: 978-1-4165-3585-0
10 Digit ISBN: 1-4165-3585-3

11 10 9 8 7 6 5 4 3 2

For information regarding special discounts for bulk purchases, please contact Simon & Schuster Special Sales at 1-800-456-6798 or business@simonandschuster.com.

Compiled by Criswell Freeman
Edited by Between the Lines
Cover design by Stephanie D. Walker & Lisa Betts
Interior design by Bart Dawson

When God thought of Mother,
He must have laughed with satisfaction—
so rich, so deep, so full of power
and beauty was the conception.

—Henry Ward Beecher

Introduction

If you're reading this book, you probably answer to "Mom," "Mother," "Mommy," or some variation thereof—and if so, congratulations. You have much to be thankful for.

Motherhood is a priceless gift from God, yet it's also an unrelenting responsibility. The words on these pages are intended to remind you that when it comes to the tough job of being a responsible mom, you and God, working together, are destined to do great things for your kids and for the world.

Perhaps you received this book as a gift from your child or your husband. Or perhaps, amid the hustle and bustle of your day, you managed to pick up a copy of your own accord. Either way, you'll be blessed if you take to heart the ideas gathered here.

As a mother, you know how overwhelming your job can be, when more is required of you than you have the time or energy to give, when time to yourself is a luxury, if not an impossibility. But when you take the time to slow down long enough to spend quiet moments with your Creator, you avail yourself of the peace and abundance God offers to those who invite Him into their hearts. Sort of like getting a hug from your heavenly Father.

And moms know all about hugs. They know that hugs can take several forms. Physical hugs may range from a polite pat on the back to the full-contact bear hug. But other kinds of hugs, while more subtle, can be just as effective. You can share emotional hugs when you offer a kind word to a friend or family member. You can share a spiritual hug when you bow your head and pray with your child. You can share a hug of faith when you offer a word of encouragement to someone who is discouraged or fearful. In short, you can share feelings of love and affection through your words, through your deeds, and through your prayers. And hopefully you receive all kinds of hugs too!

This book contains 365 devotional readings to help you prepare your heart and mind for the opportunities to give—and to receive—as many hugs as possible throughout the day. You'll find topics of particular interest to you, a mom living in an uncertain world. If you take the time to meditate on these devotional readings, you'll be reminded of God's love and of His promises.

You'll also be warmed by the Thank-You Hug that welcomes each new month. Take a moment to receive this gift of thanks as a hug of inspiration for your heart. And finally, you'll find a few lined pages at the end of the book, set aside for you to jot down your own inspirations as you read. Your recorded insights and meditations will inspire your soul as you write and as you reread.

May these pages be a blessing to you, and may you, in turn, be a blessing to your family, to your friends, and to all those whom God has seen fit to place along your path.

January

A Thank-You Hug for Mom

Dear Mom,

As the new year begins, we pause to think about the years that have passed—and about all you've done for us. You've worked so hard and made so many sacrifices that we cannot begin to thank you for each and every act of kindness. You've simply given us more gifts than we could ever count. But even if we can't count your gifts, we know why you gave them—because of your love for us. And don't ever forget, Mom, that we love you too . . . now and forever.

Happy New Year!

*May he grant your heart's desires
and make all your plans succeed.*
Psalm 20:4 NLT

Welcome, Mom, to the new year. This year, like every year, is brimming with opportunities for you and your loved ones. Your job is to search for those opportunities, to pick out the best ones, and to make the most of them. And with God's help, you can.

When you summon the courage to dream big dreams, and when you do the hard work needed to make those dreams come true, God doesn't stand idly by; He pitches in and helps. And of this you can be sure: with you and God working together, the possibilities for the coming year are limitless.

So as you plan for the next 365 days, dream big, plan big, and ask God to do big things. Trust your hopes, not your fears . . . and get ready for things to happen. Really big things.

*Start by doing what's necessary, then what's possible,
and suddenly you are doing the impossible.*
Saint Francis of Assisi

Mother Knew Best

The wise people will shine like the brightness of the sky.
Those who teach others to live right
will shine like stars forever and ever.
Daniel 12:3 NCV

Young Wilma's doctors offered a pessimistic diagnosis: they said that as a result of her polio, she might never walk again—but Wilma's mother believed otherwise. Yet she understood that her daughter couldn't receive adequate treatment in their small Tennessee town, because blacks weren't welcome at the local hospital. What to do? Wilma's mother had the answer: she and her little girl would ride the bus, an hour and a half each way, to Nashville for treatment.

First Wilma learned to hobble about with the help of crutches, then with braces, and finally she managed to walk on her own. But neither Wilma nor her mother would be satisfied until Wilma learned to run. And run she did.

Wilma Rudolph, Olympic champion and polio survivor, became the most accomplished and admired sprinter of her generation because of her determination, her courage, her faith, and her mother . . . but not necessarily in that order.

The woman is the heart of the home.
Mother Teresa

The Futility of Worry

Worry is a heavy load.
Proverbs 12:25 NCV

If you're like most mothers, it's simply a fact of life: from time to time, you worry. You worry about children, about health, about finances, about safety, and about countless other challenges in life, some great and some small.

When you stop to think about it, you'll probably agree that most of the things you worry about never come to pass. In fact, worry is simply the mind's way of cluttering up today's opportunities with memories of troubles that have already passed—or fears about troubles that may never come.

So why not let yesterday and tomorrow fend for themselves? Focus instead on this day, and turn your worries over to a Power greater than yourself. Spend your valuable time and energy solving the problems you can fix today . . . while trusting God to take care of the rest.

Concern should drive us into action
and not into depression.
Karen Horney

God's Perspective . . . and Yours

*Since you have been raised to new life with Christ,
set your sights on the realities of heaven, where Christ sits
at God's right hand in the place of honor and power.*
Colossians 3:1 NLT

Even if you're the world's most thoughtful mom, you may, from time to time, lose perspective—it happens on those days when life seems off balance and the pressures of motherhood seem overwhelming. What's needed is a fresh perspective, a restored sense of balance . . . and God.

If a temporary loss of perspective has left you worried, exhausted, or both, it's time to readjust your thought patterns. Negative thoughts are habit forming; thankfully, so are positive ones. With practice, you can form the habit of focusing on God's priorities and your possibilities. When you do, you'll spend less time fretting about your challenges and more time praising God for His gifts.

So today and every day, pray for a sense of balance and perspective. And remember: your thoughts are powerful things, so handle them with care.

*Instead of being frustrated and overwhelmed by
all that is going on in our world, go to the Lord
and ask Him to give you His eternal perspective.*
Kay Arthur

As the World Grows Louder

Be silent before the LORD and wait expectantly for Him.
Psalm 37:7 HCSB

The world seems to grow louder day by day, and our senses seem to be invaded at every turn. If we allow the distractions of a clamorous society to separate us from God's peace, we do ourselves a profound disservice. Our task is to carve out moments of silence in a world filled with noise.

If we are to maintain righteous minds and compassionate hearts, we must take time each day for prayer and for meditation. We must make ourselves still in the presence of our Creator. We must quiet our minds and our hearts so that we might sense God's will and His love.

Has the hectic pace of life robbed you, at least in part, of the joys of motherhood? If so, it's time to reorder your priorities and your life. Nothing is more important than the time you spend with your heavenly Father. So be still and claim the genuine peace that is found in the silent moments you spend with God.

Deepest communion with God is beyond words,
on the other side of silence.
Madeleine L'Engle

Life on Its Own Terms

People may make plans in their minds,
but the LORD decides what they will do.
Proverbs 16:9 NCV

Sometimes we must accept life on its terms, not our own. Life has a way of unfolding, not as we will, but as it wills. And sometimes there's precious little we can do to change things.

When events transpire that are beyond our control, we have a choice: we can either learn the art of acceptance, or we can make ourselves miserable as we struggle to change the unchangeable.

We must entrust the things we cannot change to God. Once we've done so, we can prayerfully and faithfully tackle the important work He has placed before us: doing something about the things we can change . . . and doing it sooner rather than later.

Can you summon the courage and the wisdom to accept life on its own terms? If so, Mom, you and your family will most certainly be rewarded for your inner strength and good judgment.

I pray hard, work hard, and leave the rest to God.
Florence Griffith Joyner

Beyond the Frustrations

*Put away all the following: anger, wrath, malice, slander,
and filthy language from your mouth.*
Colossians 3:8 HCSB

Motherhood is tremendously rewarding, but every mother knows that it can be, at times, frustrating. No family is perfect, and even the most loving mother's patience can, on occasion, wear thin.

Your temper is either your master or your servant. Either you control it or it controls you. And the extent to which you allow anger to rule your life will determine, to a surprising degree, the quality of your relationships with others and your relationship with God.

If you've allowed anger to become a regular visitor at your house, pray for wisdom, patience, and a heart that is so filled with forgiveness that it has no room for bitterness. The next time you're tempted to lose your temper over the minor inconveniences in life, don't. Turn away from anger, hatred, bitterness, and regret. Turn instead to God. He's waiting . . . patiently . . . with open arms.

*To handle yourself, use your head. To handle others,
use your heart. Anger is only one letter short of danger.*
Eleanor Roosevelt

The Right Kind of Example

*Be an example to the believers in word, in conduct,
in love, in spirit, in faith, in purity.*
1 Timothy 4:12 NKJV

It would be easy to teach our kids everything they need to know about life if we could teach them with words alone. But we can't. Our kids hear some of the things we say, but they watch everything we do.

As parents, we are unforgettable role models for our children and our grandchildren. As they observe our lives and the choices we have made, they'll see what rewards come to those who worship God and obey His commandments.

Is your faith demonstrated in the example you set for your children? If so, you will be blessed—and so will they. So today, as you fulfill your many responsibilities, remember that your family is watching . . . and so, for that matter, is God.

*The mother is and must be, whether she knows it
or not, the greatest, strongest,
and most lasting teacher her children have.*
Hannah Whitall Smith

The Best Day to Celebrate

Celebrate God all day, every day. I mean, revel in him!
Philippians 4:4 MSG

What is the best day to celebrate life? This one! Today and every day should be a day of prayer and celebration as you consider the joys and opportunities of loving and caring for your family.

What do you expect from the day ahead? Are you an optimistic mom who's expecting God to do wonderful things for you and yours, or are you living beneath a cloud of apprehension and doubt? The answer to this question will affect the quality of your day . . . and the quality of your family life. After all, if you can't find ways to celebrate your family, perhaps it's time to pay closer attention.

So as you plan for the day ahead, Mom, remember that it's up to you to make sure celebration is woven into the very fabric of your life. But what greater joy than when those you love join in the celebration with you!

If you can forgive the person you were, accept the person you are, and believe in the person you will become, you are headed for joy. So celebrate your life.
Barbara Johnson

Pockets of Joy

I will thank you, LORD, with all my heart;
I will tell of all the marvelous things you have done.
I will be filled with joy because of you.
I will sing praises to your name, O Most High.
Psalm 9:1–2 NLT

Have you experienced real joy lately—the kind of joy that makes your heart soar? Hopefully so, because you're a mom loved by God; this is what He desires for you.

Should you expect to be a joy-filled mother twenty-four hours a day, seven days a week, from this moment on? No. But you can (and should) experience pockets of joy—moments when you're wonderfully overwhelmed by the immensity of God's gifts.

How can you find the kind of joy that lifts your heart and fills your soul? Start by consulting your heavenly Father each day. Then do all the good you can, wherever you can, whenever you can. Resolve to love everybody, starting with the people who dwell under your roof. And spend a significant portion of every day thanking your Creator for His blessings. When you do these things, your joys will be multiplied and your life will be blessed.

Taking joy in life is a woman's best cosmetic.
Rosalind Russell

Listening to God

The one who is from God listens to God's words.
This is why you don't listen,
because you are not from God.
John 8:47 HCSB

Sometimes God speaks loudly and clearly. More often He speaks in a quiet voice—and if you're wise, you'll be listening carefully when He does. But to do that, you'll need to carve out quiet moments each day to quiet your soul and sense His presence.

Can you quiet yourself long enough to listen for your heavenly Father's direction? Are you a mother who is attuned to the subtle instructions of your God-given "intuition"? Are you willing to pray sincerely and then wait quietly for your Creator's response? Hopefully so. Usually God refrains from sending messages via stone tablets or city billboards. Most of the time He communicates in subtler ways. If you sincerely desire to hear His voice, you must listen carefully . . . and you must do so by bringing stillness to every corner of your willing heart.

Half an hour of listening is essential except when one is very busy. Then, a full hour is needed.
Saint Francis de Sales

Picking and Choosing

It is the LORD your God you must follow,
and him you must revere. Keep his commands
and obey him; serve him and hold fast to him.
Deuteronomy 13:4 NIV

At one time or another we all face a similar temptation—the temptation to follow some of God's rules and disregard others. But if we're wise, we won't pick and choose among the Bible's commands. We'll do our best to obey them all, not just the ones that are easy or convenient. When we do, we can expect to be blessed by our loving, heavenly Father.

Today, Mom, take every step of your journey with God as your traveling companion. Read His Word and take it seriously. Support only those activities that further your spiritual growth. Be a positive example to your children, to your friends, to your neighbors, and to your community. Then prepare yourself for the countless blessings God has promised to all those who follow Him wholeheartedly.

Keep true, and never be ashamed of doing right;
decide on what you think is right, and stick to it.
George Eliot

Planning (and Working) for the Future

First plant your fields; then build your barn.
Proverbs 24:27 MSG

Are you willing to plan for the future—and are you willing to work diligently to bring those plans to fruition? The book of Proverbs teaches that the plans of hardworking people (like you) will be rewarded.

If you want to reap a bountiful harvest from life, you must plan for the future while entrusting the final outcome to God. You also need to do your part to make the future better (by working dutifully) while acknowledging the sovereignty of God's hand over all things—including your own plans and efforts.

Are you one of those moms who's in a hurry for success to arrive at your family's doorstep? Don't be. Instead, work diligently, plan thoughtfully, and wait patiently. Remember that you're not the only one working on your behalf; God, too, is at work. And with Him as your partner, your ultimate success is guaranteed.

Allow your dreams a place in your prayers and plans.
God-given dreams can help you move
into the future He is preparing for you.
Barbara Johnson

When God Speaks to Your Heart

*They show that in their hearts they know
what is right and wrong.*
Romans 2:15 NCV

Hey, Mom, when God speaks through that small, quiet voice that He has placed in your heart, are you ready and willing to listen? Hopefully so; after all, God has equipped you with a conscience—a clear sense of right and wrong—and He intends for you to use it.

But sometimes, especially in times of crisis, it's hard to trust your own insights because your inner voice—God's internal guidance system—can be drowned out by fear, worry, anxiety, or confusion.

If you're facing a difficult question or an important decision, your most trusted advisor (aside from God's Word) may be that still, small voice God has placed within you. So listen to your conscience, and pay careful attention to the things you hear. God is probably trying to get His message through to you, but He may not be willing to shout.

*Trust your hunches. Hunches are usually based on
facts filed away below the conscious. But be warned:
don't confuse hunches with wishful thinking.*
Dr. Joyce Brothers

What You Choose to Make of Life

*We are hoping for something we do not have yet,
and we are waiting for it patiently.*
Romans 8:25 NCV

You've heard the saying "Life is what you make it." And although that statement may seem trite, it's also true. You can choose to go through life filled with frustration and fear, or you can choose contentment and peace. Of course, you can't control what happens in life. But you can choose what to make of it, and your choices will depend on your attitude.

What's your attitude today, Mom? And what's the prevailing sentiment of the people who live under your roof? Are you fearful, angry, bored, or worried? Are you pessimistic, perplexed, pained, and perturbed? If so, it's time for an attitude adjustment.

God created you (and your family) in His own image, and He wants you to experience joy, contentment, peace, and abundance. But He won't force you to experience these things; you must claim them for yourself. And when is the best time to start reaping the rewards of a right attitude? Right now, of course!

On the human chessboard, all moves are possible.
Miriam Schiff

Getting Better

Even a child is known by his doings, whether his work
be pure, and whether it be right.
Proverbs 20:11 KJV

How does God intend for us to work? Does He reward mediocrity, or does He intend for us to work diligently? The answer is obvious. In God's economy hard work is rewarded and sloppy work is not. Yet sometimes we may seek ease over excellence. We may be tempted to take shortcuts when God intends that we walk the straight and narrow path.

Today, Mom, be sure to do good work. Wherever you find yourself, whatever your job description, do your work—and do it with all your heart. When you do, you'll be a marvelous example to your children, and as an added perk, you'll likely win the recognition of your peers. But more importantly, God will bless your efforts and use you in ways that only He can predict. So go about your tasks with focus and dedication. And leave the outcome to God.

The secret of joy in work
is contained in one word: excellence.
To know how to do something well is to enjoy it.
Pearl S. Buck

Mountain-Moving Faith

*I assure you: If anyone says to this mountain,
"Be lifted up and thrown into the sea," and does not
doubt in his heart, but believes that what he says
will happen, it will be done for him.*
Mark 11:23 HCSB

Are you a mother whose faith is evident for all to see? Do you trust God's promises without reservation, or do you question His promises without hesitation?

Every life—including yours—is a series of successes and failures, celebrations and disappointments, joys and sorrows. But every step of the way, through every triumph and tragedy, God will stand by your side and strengthen you . . . if you have faith in Him.

Jesus taught His disciples that if they had faith, they could move mountains. You can too, and so can your family. But you must have faith. So today and every day, trust your heavenly Father, give thanks for the sacrifice of His Son . . . and then let the mountain-moving begin.

*Seeds of faith are always within us; sometimes it takes
a crisis to nourish and encourage their growth.*
Susan L. Taylor

Asking Often

For everyone who asks receives, and the one who searches finds, and to the one who knocks, the door will be opened.
Matthew 7:8 HCSB

If you need God's help, ask Him for it! When you ask sincerely—and repeatedly—He will answer your request.

How often do you ask God for His guidance and His wisdom? Occasionally? Intermittently? Whenever you experience a crisis? Hopefully, you've acquired the habit of asking for God's assistance early and often. And hopefully, you've learned to seek His guidance in every aspect of your life.

God has promised that when you ask for His help, He will not withhold it. So ask. Ask Him to meet the needs you have today. Ask Him to lead you, protect you, and correct you. And trust the answers He gives.

God stands at the door and waits. When you knock, He opens. When you ask, He answers. Your task is simply to seek His guidance prayerfully, confidently, and often.

It is our part to seek, His to grant what we ask;
our part to make a beginning, His to bring it to
completion; our part to offer what we can,
His to finish what we cannot.
Saint Jerome

Where the Heart Is

You must choose for yourselves today
whom you will serve. . . . As for me and my family,
we will serve the LORD.
Joshua 24:15 NCV

In a letter to his wife, Martha, George Washington wrote: "I should enjoy more real happiness in one month with you at home than I have the most distant prospect of finding happiness abroad, if my stay were to be seven times seven years." Thoughtful men and women agree: home is not only where the heart is; it's also where the happiness is.

Your family is your most prized earthly possession; it is a priceless, one-of-a-kind gift from God. Treasure it, Mom, and protect it. That little band of men, women, kids, babies, dogs, cats, hamsters, and goldfish is a priceless treasure on temporary loan from the Father above. Give thanks to the Giver for the gift of family . . . and enjoy them like the treasures they are.

When you look at your life,
the greatest happiness is family happiness.
Dr. Joyce Brothers

Building Character

People with integrity have firm footing,
but those who follow crooked paths will slip and fall.
Proverbs 10:9 NLT

Wise mothers teach the importance of character. Character doesn't spring up overnight; it grows gradually over a lifetime. It is the sum of every right decision, every honest word, every noble thought, and every heartfelt prayer. Character is a precious thing—difficult to build but easy to tear down; wise mothers value it and protect it at all costs . . . and they encourage their children to do the same.

Are you serious about teaching your children the importance of integrity, through both your words and your deeds? Of course you are. And so is God. So here's the challenge: Consider God to be your partner as you teach your children. Then, with no further delay, let the character building begin . . . today.

Don't mistake personality for character.
Wilma Askinas

Claiming Contentment in a Discontented World

*Satisfy us in the morning with your unfailing love,
that we may sing for joy and be glad all our days.*
Psalm 90:14 NIV

Everywhere we turn, or so it seems, the world promises us contentment and happiness. We're bombarded by messages offering us the "good life" if only we will purchase products and services that are designed to provide happiness, success, and contentment. But the contentment the world offers is fleeting and incomplete. Thankfully, the contentment God offers is all-encompassing and everlasting.

Happiness depends less on our circumstances than on our thoughts. When we turn our thoughts to God, to His gifts, and to His glorious creation, we experience the joy God intends for His children. But when we focus on the negative aspects of life—or when we disobey God's commandments—we cause ourselves needless suffering.

So here's a strategy for happiness that's proven and true: claim the spiritual abundance God offers His children . . . and keep claiming it, Mom, day by glorious day, for as long as you live.

Joy is the serious business of heaven.
C. S. Lewis

Developing Discipline

*God hasn't invited us into a disorderly, unkempt life
but into something holy and beautiful—
as beautiful on the inside as the outside.*
1 Thessalonians 4:7 MSG

God's Word makes it clear: we are instructed to be disciplined, diligent, moderate, and mature. But the world often tempts us to behave in other ways. It seems every day we're faced with powerful incentives to conduct ourselves in ways that are undisciplined, immoderate, and imprudent.

We live in a world in which leisure is glorified and misbehavior is glamorized. We inhabit a society where sloppy is in and neatness is out. We watch as the media often put bad behavior on a pedestal. But God has other plans. He did not create us for lives of mischief or mediocrity; He created us for far greater things.

As you know, Mom, God rewards diligence and righteousness—and He often does so sooner rather than later. So teach your children well . . . and teach them now.

*It doesn't matter what you're trying to accomplish.
It's all a matter of discipline.*
Wilma Rudolph

Sharing Words of Encouragement

Good people's words will help many others.
Proverbs 10:21 NCV

The words we speak have the power to do great good or great harm. If we speak words of encouragement and hope, we can lift others up. And that's exactly what God commands us to do!

Sometimes, when we feel uplifted and secure, it's easy to speak kind words. Other times, when we're discouraged or tired, we can scarcely summon the energy to pick ourselves up, much less anyone else. Yet God desires that we speak words of kindness, wisdom, and truth, no matter our circumstances, no matter our emotions.

So here's something worth remembering, Mom: when you share the gift of encouragement, you share a priceless gift with the world—and because you are a mother who has been richly blessed by the Creator, that's precisely what you should do.

An effort made for the happiness of others
lifts us above ourselves.
Lydia Maria Child

Attitude of Gratitude

*Everything created by God is good, and nothing
is to be rejected, if it is received with gratitude; for it is
sanctified by means of the word of God and prayer.*
1 Timothy 4:4–5 NASB

For most mothers, life is busy and complicated. But no one needs to tell you that. You already know firsthand that motherhood is one of the toughest jobs on earth (thankfully, it's also one of the most rewarding jobs on earth).

Sometimes, amid the rush and crush of the daily grind, you may find it easy to lose sight of God and His blessings. But when you forget to slow down and say thank you to your Maker, you're unintentionally robbing yourself of His peace and His joy.

Even if you're an overworked mom, instead of ignoring God, take time to praise Him many times each day. Then, with gratitude in your heart, you can face the day's duties with the perspective and power that only He can provide.

*A sense of gratitude for God's presence in our lives
will help open our eyes to what He has done in the past
and what He will do in the future.*
Emilie Barnes

Time to Forgive

If you forgive people their wrongdoing,
your heavenly Father will forgive you as well.
But if you don't forgive people,
your Father will not forgive your wrongdoing.
Matthew 6:14–15 HCSB

Bitterness is a roadblock on the path God has laid out for your life. If you allow yourself to become resentful, discouraged, envious, or embittered, you will become spiritually "stuck." But if you obey God's Word and forgive those who have harmed you, you'll experience God's peace as you follow His path.

If you seek to live in accordance with God's will for your life—and you should—then you will live in accordance with His commands. And don't forget: for followers of God, forgiving others is never optional; it's required.

God will use you in wonderful, unexpected ways if you let Him. But the decision to seek God's plan and to follow it is yours and yours alone, Mom. Don't let bitterness, or any other transgression, get in the way.

To hold on to hate and resentments is to
throw a monkey wrench into the machinery of life.
E. Stanley Jones

God's Attentiveness

*The eyes of the LORD range throughout the earth
to show Himself strong for those whose hearts
are completely His.*
2 Chronicles 16:9 HCSB

God is not distant, and He is not disinterested. On the contrary, your heavenly Father is attentive to your needs. In fact, God knows precisely what you need and when you need it. But He still wants to hear it from you. He wants to talk with you, and if you're wise, you'll want to talk to Him too.

Do you have questions you can't answer? Ask for guidance from your Creator. Do you sincerely seek the gifts of everlasting love and eternal life? Accept God's gift of grace. Whatever your need, Mom, no matter how great or small, pray about it. Instead of waiting for mealtimes or bedtimes, pray always, and never lose heart. Remember: God is here, and He's ready to talk with you now. So please don't make Him wait another moment.

*Our future may look fearfully intimidating,
yet we can look up to the Engineer of the Universe,
confident that nothing escapes His attention
or slips out of the control of those strong hands.*
Elisabeth Elliot

When Your Courage Is Tested

Be strong and courageous,
all you who put your hope in the LORD.
Psalm 31:24 HCSB

Even the most optimistic person on the planet may find her courage tested by the inevitable disappointments and tragedies of life. After all, we live in a world filled with uncertainty, hardship, sickness, and danger. Old Man Trouble, it seems, is never far away.

When we focus upon our fears and our doubts, we'll find many reasons to lie awake at night and fret about the uncertainties of the coming day. A better strategy, of course, is to focus not on our fears but on our God.

So, Mom, here's a hint: don't dwell on worst-case scenarios, and don't focus too intently on your fears. Instead, trust God's plan and His eternal love for you. And remember: whatever the size of your challenge, God is bigger.

I have found the perfect antidote for fear. Whenever it
sticks up its ugly face, I clobber it with prayer.
Dale Evans Rogers

Always Growing

*Whenever trouble comes your way,
let it be an opportunity for joy. For when your faith
is tested, your endurance has a chance to grow.
So let it grow, for when your endurance is fully developed,
you will be strong in character and ready for anything.*
James 1:2–4 NLT

As a mother you have a profound responsibility to be a positive role model for your children. So here's a question that should make you pause and think: do you want your kids to keep growing intellectually, emotionally, and spiritually? If you answered yes (which, undoubtedly, you did), you'll have to keep growing too. To set a positive example for your children, you must continue to expand your horizons through every stage of life.

Growth can be painful; it's sometimes earned at a very high price; but for thoughtful women like you, personal growth is always worth the cost.

Today, Mom, you will encounter circumstances, perhaps troubling circumstances, that will offer you opportunities to grow . . . or not. Choose growth—it's the highest and best way to live.

*You've got to continue to grow,
or you're just like last night's cornbread: stale and dry.*
Loretta Lynn

Seeking His Will

Teach me to do Your will, for You are my God;
Your Spirit is good. Lead me in the land of uprightness.
Psalm 143:10 NKJV

The book of Judges tells the story of Deborah, the brave woman who helped lead the army of Israel to victory over the Canaanites. Deborah was a judge and a prophet, a woman called by God to lead her people. And when she answered God's call, she was rewarded with one of the great victories of Old Testament times.

Like Deborah, all of us are called to serve our Creator. And like Deborah, we may sometimes find ourselves facing trials that can make us tremble in the very depths of our souls. What should we do? We, like Deborah, should entrust our lives to God completely and without reservation. When we do, He will give us the strength to meet any challenge, the courage to face any trial, and the wisdom to live in His righteousness and in His peace.

Our heavenly Father knows to place us where we may
learn lessons impossible anywhere else.
He has neither misplaced nor displaced us.
Elisabeth Elliot

Your Child's Most Important Teacher

Impress these words of Mine on your hearts and souls. . . .
Teach them to your children, talking about them when you
sit in your house and when you walk along the road,
when you lie down and when you get up.
Deuteronomy 11:18–19 HCSB

Each child is unique, but every child is similar in this respect: he or she is a priceless gift from the Father above. And with God's gift of a child comes immense responsibility for moms (and dads).

Even on those difficult days when the house is in an uproar and the laundry is piled high, wise mothers never forget their overriding goal: shaping young minds and hearts. The best moms shape those minds with love, with discipline, and with God.

Our children are our most precious resource. May we, as responsible and dedicated mothers, pray for our children here at home and for children around the world. Every child is God's child. May we, as loving parents, behave—and teach—accordingly.

We always need to be on the lookout for those teachable
moments with our children—spontaneous lessons
that appear in the side yard, the laundry room,
and the grocery store.
Susan Card

A Simple Smile

What a relief it is to see your friendly smile.
It is like seeing the smile of God!
Genesis 33:10 NLT

A smile is nourishment for the heart, and laughter is medicine for the soul—but sometimes, amid the stresses of the day, we forget to take our medicine. Instead of viewing our world with a mixture of optimism and humor, we allow worries and distractions to rob us of the joy God wants us to know in our lives.

So next time you find yourself dwelling on the negatives of life, refocus your attention on things positive, and smile. When you find yourself falling prey to the blight of pessimism, stop and smile; it'll help you turn your thoughts around. With a loving God as your protector, and with a loving family to support you, you've got plenty to smile about.

So smile, Mom! It'll do you—and everyone around you—a world of good.

If you could choose one characteristic
that would get you through life,
choose a sense of humor.
Jennifer Jones

February

A Thank-You Hug for Mom

Dear Mom,

You have always nurtured our family, and we've noticed. Even when we've made mistakes, and even when we've been difficult to live with, you've always been there for us. Raising a family is incredibly hard work, but you have been incredibly faithful. And we are incredibly grateful.

Imperfect Parenting

He whose ear listens to the life-giving reproof
will dwell among the wise.
Proverbs 15:31 NASB

If you're trying to be a perfect mother, it's time to give yourself a reality check. No matter how hard you try, you can't be perfect, and when you make mistakes (as you most certainly will), you should be quick to forgive yourself . . . and just as quick to learn the lessons that can be gleaned from your experience.

No parent is perfect. And even the best children are far from perfect too. Thus, we are imperfect parents raising imperfect children, and, as a result, mistakes are bound to happen.

You and your loved ones should view mistakes as opportunities to reassess how well you're following God's will for your lives. And while you're at it, remember to view life's inevitable disappointments as powerful opportunities to learn more—more about yourselves, more about your circumstances, and more about your world.

Parenthood is the world's most intensive course in love.
Polly Berrien Berends

Full Confidence

*May the God of hope fill you with all joy
and peace as you trust in him, so that you may overflow
with hope by the power of the Holy Spirit.*
Romans 15:13 NIV

Are you a confident mom, or do you live under a cloud of uncertainty and doubt? The answer to this question will affect how you view your family, your future, your work, and your world. As the saying goes, "Attitude determines altitude." The higher your hopes, the higher you're likely to soar.

Yet even the most confident moms will encounter situations that raise doubts and fears. You're no exception. But when you see those inevitable storm clouds on the horizon, don't lose hope. After all, you're part of a loving family; you possess unique talents; you have the determination and the courage to tackle your problems; and you are always in the presence of the Ultimate Partner. With God and family by your side, you have every reason to be confident.

*To know God as He really is—in His essential nature
and character—is to arrive at a citadel of peace that
circumstances may storm, but can never capture.*
Catherine Marshall

Continuing to Seek His Purpose

Let us not become weary in doing good,
for at the proper time we will reap a harvest
if we do not give up.
Galatians 6:9 NIV

As you continue to seek God's purpose for your life, you'll undoubtedly experience your fair share of disappointments, detours, false starts, and failures. When you do, don't become discouraged: God's not finished with you yet.

The old saying is as true today as it was when it was first spoken: "Life is a marathon, not a sprint." That's why wise travelers (and wise mothers) select a traveling companion who never tires and never falters. That partner, of course, is your heavenly Father.

Are you tired, Mom? Ask God for strength. Are you discouraged? Believe in His promises. Have faith that you play an important role in God's great plan for His big, beautiful world—because you do.

Whether you have twenty years left, ten years,
one year, one month, one day, or just one hour,
there is something very important God wants you to do
that can add to His kingdom and your blessing.
Bill Bright

Perseverance

If you do nothing in a difficult time,
your strength is limited.
Proverbs 24:10 HCSB

Perhaps more than any other job, motherhood requires energy, courage, perseverance, determination . . . and, of course, an unending supply of motherly love. Whew!

OK, Mom, be honest. Are your wheels spinning so fast you're afraid the lug nuts might melt? Are you so busy that sleep has become a luxury? Do you feel too weary to walk on and too tired to care? If so, turn to God for strength. Spend some time meditating on His promises. And hang in there. Keep working as if everything depended on you, but pray as if everything depended on God.

With His help you will find the strength to be the kind of mom who makes her heavenly Father beam with pride. And who knows, maybe sometime soon you can even get eight hours' sleep!

Before you begin anything, remind yourself that difficulties
and delays quite impossible to foresee are ahead.
You can only see one thing clearly, and that is your goal.
Form a mental vision of that first, and cling to it
through thick and thin.
Kathleen Norris

First Things First

First pay attention to me, and then relax.
Now you can take it easy—you're in good hands.
Proverbs 1:33 MSG

First things first." These words are easy to say but hard to put into practice. For busy mothers living in a demanding world, putting first things first can be difficult indeed. Why? Because so many people are expecting so many things from you!

If you're having trouble prioritizing your day, perhaps you've been trying to organize your life according to your own plans, not God's. Here's a better strategy: take your daily obligations and place them in the hands of the One who created you. To do so, you'll need to prioritize your day according to God's commands, not others' demands; and you must seek His will and His wisdom in all matters. Then you can face the day with the assurance that the same God who orders the universe will help you order your life.

Does God care about all the responsibilities we have
to juggle in our daily lives? Of course. But he cares more
that our lives demonstrate balance, the ability to discern
what is essential and give ourselves fully to it.
Penelope Stokes

His Answer to Our Guilt

*If my people who are called by my name will humble
themselves and pray and seek my face
and turn from their wicked ways, I will hear from heaven
and will forgive their sins and heal their land.*
2 Chronicles 7:14 NLT

All of us (even those "almost perfect" moms) make mistakes—sometimes big mistakes. And when we fall short of our own expectations, or God's, we may experience intense feelings of guilt. But God has an antidote for our guilt: His forgiveness. When we confess our mistakes and receive God's forgiveness, then we are also free to forgive ourselves. And we can also learn from our mistakes and stop repeating them.

Are you troubled by feelings of guilt or regret? If so, put yourself back on the right path by putting an end to your misbehavior and asking your heavenly Father for His forgiveness. When you do, He will forgive you completely and without reservation. Then—and this is important—it's time to forgive yourself just as God has forgiven you: thoroughly and unconditionally.

*If we do not deal with sin, our spiritual lives
become stagnant and we lose our attractiveness
and usefulness to God.*
Anne Graham Lotz

The Power of Habits

*Change your hearts and lives because
the kingdom of heaven is near.*
Matthew 3:2 NCV

You've heard it said on many occasions: first you make your habits, and then your habits make you. Some habits will inevitably bring you closer to God; other habits will lead you away from the path He has chosen for you. If you sincerely desire to improve your spiritual health, you must honestly examine the habits that make up the fabric of your day. And you must abandon any habits that are harming you. If you want to improve your life, improve your habits.

Mom, with God by your side, you have the power to form healthier habits. And those habits are powerful tools for improving your life—for creating a stronger, healthier you. Ask God to help you take control of your life today, and then put your new habits to work for you.

Begin to be now what you will be hereafter.
Saint Jerome

The Right Kinds of Risk

*Be sure to stay busy and plant a variety of crops,
for you never know which will grow—perhaps they all will.*
Ecclesiastes 11:6 NLT

As we consider the uncertainties of the future, we're confronted with a powerful temptation: the temptation to "play it safe." Unwilling to move mountains, we fret over molehills. Unwilling to entertain great hopes for tomorrow, we focus on the unfairness of today. Unwilling to trust God completely, we take timid half steps when God wants us to take giant leaps.

Today, Mom, ask God for the courage to step beyond the boundaries of your doubts. Ask Him to guide you to a place where you can realize your full potential—a place where you're free from the fear of failure. Ask Him to do His part, and promise Him that you will do your part. Don't ask Him to lead you to a safe place; ask Him to lead you to the right place. And remember . . . those two places are seldom the same.

*Failure after long perseverance is much grander
than never to have a striving good enough
to be called a failure.*
George Eliot

Giving Thanks

Bless the LORD, O my soul, and forget not all his benefits.
Psalm 103:2 KJV

As you begin another day, have you stopped to thank God for His blessings? Have you offered Him your heartfelt prayers and your wholehearted praise? If so, you're a wise woman indeed. If not, it's time to slow down and offer a prayer of thanksgiving to the One who has given you life on earth and life eternal.

If you are a thoughtful mother, you'll also be a thankful mother. After all, God has blessed you with a loving family, which in itself is a gift beyond compare. But God's gifts don't stop there. He has blessed you in countless other ways too.

When you stop to think about it, you'll realize that you owe the Creator much more than you can ever repay. For starters, realize that you owe Him your enduring gratitude. So thank the Giver of all good gifts . . . and keep thanking Him, today, tomorrow, and forever.

The best way to show my gratitude to God
is to accept everything, even my problems, with joy.
Mother Teresa

When Your Family Has Questions

The counsel of the LORD standeth for ever,
the thoughts of his heart to all generations.
Psalm 33:11 KJV

When you and your loved ones have questions that you simply can't answer, whom do you ask? When you face difficult decisions, to whom do you turn for counsel? To friends? to mentors? to family members? Or do you turn first to the ultimate source of wisdom? For the answers to life's big questions, start with God and His Word.

God's wisdom stands forever, and His Word is a light for every generation. Make it your light as well. Use the Bible as a compass on your journey. Use it as the yardstick by which your behavior (and your children's behavior) is measured. And as you carefully consult the pages of God's Word, prayerfully ask Him to reveal the wisdom you need. When you and your family members take your questions to God, He will not turn you away; He will, instead, offer answers that are tested and true. Your job is simply to ask, to listen, and to trust.

We don't do drugs, drink, or use profanity.
Instead, we instill morals and values in my boys
by raising them with a love of God and a love
and respect for themselves and all people.
Anita Baker

New Beginnings

*There is a time for everything,
and a season for every activity under heaven.*
Ecclesiastes 3:1 NIV

Each new day offers countless opportunities to serve God, to seek His will, and to obey His teachings. But each day also offers countless opportunities to stray from God's commandments and to wander far from His path.

Sometimes we wander aimlessly in a wilderness of our own making, but God has better plans for us. And whenever we ask Him to renew our strength and guide our steps, He does so.

Mom, consider this day a new beginning. Think of it as a fresh start, a renewed opportunity to serve your Creator with willing hands and a loving heart. Ask God to renew your sense of purpose as He guides your steps. Today is a glorious opportunity to serve God. Seize that opportunity while you can; tomorrow may be too late.

*The world is round, and the place which may seem
like the end may also be only the beginning.*
Ivy Baker Priest

Your Priceless Treasures

*Whoever embraces one of these children as I do
embraces me, and far more than me—God who sent me.*
Mark 9:37 MSG

As a mother, you are keenly aware that God has
entrusted you with a priceless treasure from
above: your child. Every child is a wonderfully
unique, glorious gift from above—and with that gift
comes immense responsibilities.

Thoughtful mothers (like you) understand the
critical importance of raising their children with
love, with family, with discipline, and with God. By
making God a focus in the home, loving mothers
offer a priceless legacy to their children—a legacy of
hope, a legacy of love, and a legacy of wisdom.

Take time today to pray for your children. And
spend a few extra minutes praying for children around
the world. Every child is precious to God. May every
child be precious to us as well.

*Every child born into the world is a new thought of God,
an ever-fresh and radiant possibility.*
Kate Douglas Wiggin

Your Next Big Ideas

*May he give you the desire of your heart
and make all your plans succeed.*
Psalm 20:4 NIV

Ruth Handler was a partner in a small business that made plastic items and a few toys. The little company was called Mattel. But everything changed in 1959 when Ruth observed daughter Barbara pretending that paper dolls were grownups. That gave Ruth the idea for a grownup doll she would call Barbie in honor of her daughter. Since then over a billion Barbie dolls have been sold—so many, in fact, that Mattel has lost count.

Ruth Handler proved that good ideas are everywhere—we can even get them from our kids. So keep your eyes open for an idea that can change your world. When you do, you'll discover that new ideas (and fresh opportunities) are like Barbie dolls: they're simply too numerous to count.

*You don't make progress by standing on the sidelines,
whimpering and complaining.
You make progress by implementing ideas.*
Shirley Chisholm

Your Growing Faith

*For this reason we also, since the day we heard it,
do not cease to pray for you, and to ask that
you may be filled with the knowledge of His will
in all wisdom and spiritual understanding.*
Colossians 1:9 NKJV

Your relationship with God is ongoing; it unfolds day by day, and it offers countless opportunities to grow closer to Him . . . or to choose not to. As each new day unfolds, you'll be confronted with a wide range of choices: how to behave, where to direct your thoughts, with whom to associate, and what or whom to worship. Such decisions, along with many others like them, are yours and yours alone. How you choose determines how your relationship with God will unfold.

Are you continuing to grow both as a woman and as a mother, or are you resting easy in your current state of spiritual health? Hopefully, you're determined to keep growing. Your Creator deserves no less . . . and He wants nothing less for you.

*In a special way, human beings, being made
in the image of God, only become real human beings,
are only able to grow and thrive as human beings,
as they also yearn for God.*
Roberta Bondi

Beyond Doubt

*Jesus said, "Don't let your hearts be troubled.
Trust in God, and trust in me."*
John 14:1 NCV

If you've never had any doubts about your faith,
then you can stop reading this page now and skip
to the next. But if you've ever been plagued by doubts
about your faith or your God, keep reading.

Even some of the most faithful women, at times,
wrestle with discouragement and doubt. But even
when you feel far from God, God is never far from
you. He's always with you, always willing to calm the
storms of life—always willing to replace your doubts
with comfort and assurance.

Whenever you're plagued by doubts, that's
precisely the time you should seek God's presence.
Spend time establishing a deeper, more meaningful
relationship with Him. Then, Mom, you can rest
assured that in time, God will calm your fears, answer
your prayers, and restore your confidence.

*Kill the snake of doubt in your soul,
crush the worms of fear in your heart,
and mountains will move out of your way.*
Kate Seredy

No Compromise

Your love must be real. Hate what is evil,
and hold on to what is good.
Romans 12:9 NCV

This world is God's creation, and it contains the wonderful fruits of His handiwork. But it also contains countless opportunities to stray from His will. Temptations are everywhere, and the devil, it seems, never takes a day off. Your task, as a caring mother, is to do all you can to protect your family from the distractions and evil of the world. How can this be done? First you must recognize evil when you see it, and then you must fight it at every turn in the road.

When we observe life objectively—when we do so with eyes and hearts that are attuned to God's perfect Word—we can no longer be neutral observers in the battle against evil. And when we are no longer neutral, God rejoices while the devil despairs.

When good people in any country cease their vigilance
and struggle, then evil men prevail.
Pearl S. Buck

Once and for All

Be merciful, just as your Father also is merciful.
Luke 6:36 HCSB

Life would be much simpler if we could forgive people once and for all and be done with it. But forgiveness is seldom that easy. Usually the decision to forgive is straightforward . . . but the process of forgiving is more difficult. Forgiveness is a journey that requires effort, time, perseverance, and prayer.

God instructs us to treat other people exactly as we wish to be treated. And since you'll want to be forgiven for the mistakes you make (no mother is perfect, not even you), you must be willing to extend forgiveness to other people for the mistakes they make. If you can't seem to forgive someone, keep asking God to help you until you do. And you can be sure of this, Mom: if you keep asking for God's help, He will give it.

The fire of anger, if not quenched by loving forgiveness,
will spread and destroy the work of God.
Warren Wiersbe

Big Things in Store

Rejoice in hope; be patient in affliction;
be persistent in prayer.
Romans 12:12 HCSB

Do you believe God has a wonderful plan for your life? Do you believe you can discover that plan and see it fulfilled? You should, because God has marvelous things in store for you.

When it comes to the important things in life, promise yourself that you won't settle for second best. And what are the "important things"? Your faith, your family, your health, and your relationships, for starters. In each of these areas, with God's help, you can be a rip-roaring, top-drawer success.

So, Mom, if you want the best life has to offer, convince yourself that you can achieve your goals. Become sold on yourself as a child of God, and then become sold on your opportunities, sold on your abilities, and sold on God's faithfulness to you and yours. If you're sold on those things, chances are the world will soon become convinced too, and the results will be beautiful.

The first and worst of all frauds is to cheat one's self.
All sin is easy after that.
Pearl Bailey

A Wonderful Life

Thank God for this gift, his gift.
No language can praise it enough!
2 Corinthians 9:15 MSG

Each morning, as you awake and begin the new day, you're confronted with countless opportunities to serve God, to serve your family, and to serve your community. But sometimes these opportunities masquerade as burdens.

If you're trying to do many things for many people, you may feel overworked, overcommitted, and overwhelmed. But it need not be so.

When your daily to-do list starts spilling over onto second and third pages, that may be God's way of telling you to slow down and start smelling a few more roses.

So here's a prescription for a happier, healthier life: (1) View every day as a glorious opportunity; (2) Don't overcommit! (3) Help as many folks as you can, but don't burn out; (4) Don't ever stop thanking God for His blessings; and (5) Don't ever forget numbers 1 through 4.

What a wonderful life I've had!
I only wish I'd realized it sooner.
Colette

God's Plan for You

You will show me the path of life;
in Your presence is fullness of joy;
at Your right hand are pleasures forevermore.
Psalm 16:11 NKJV

God has a plan for your life. He understands that plan as thoroughly and completely as He knows you. And if you seek God's will earnestly and prayerfully, He will make His plan known to you in His own time and in His own way.

But if you sincerely seek to live in accordance with God's will for your life, you will live in accordance with His commandments. You'll study God's Word, and you'll be watchful for His signs.

Sometimes God's plan will seem unmistakably clear. But other times He may lead you through the wilderness before He directs you to the Promised Land. So, Mom, be patient and keep seeking His will for your life. When you do, you'll be amazed at the marvelous things that an all-powerful, all-knowing God can do.

God possesses infinite knowledge and an awareness which
is uniquely His. At all times, even in the midst of any type
of suffering, I can realize that He knows, loves, watches,
understands, and more than that, He has a purpose.
Billy Graham

Close to the Brokenhearted

I am the LORD who heals you.
Exodus 15:26 NCV

In time, tragedy visits all those who live long or love deeply. When our friends or family members encounter life-shattering events, we struggle to find words that might bring them comfort and support. Finding those words can be difficult, if not impossible. Sometimes all that we can do is to be with our loved ones and to pray for them, trusting that God will do the rest.

Thankfully, God promises that He is "close to the brokenhearted" (Psalm 34:18 NIV). In times of intense sadness, we can turn to Him, and we can encourage our friends and family members to do likewise. When we throw ourselves into the arms of our loving, heavenly Father, he comforts us and . . . in time . . . He heals us.

People are like stained-glass windows.
They sparkle and shine when the sun is out,
but when the darkness sets in, their true beauty is revealed
only if there is a light from within.
Elisabeth Kübler-Ross

The Joy He Has Promised

I speak these things in the world so that they may have
My joy completed in them.
John 17:13 HCSB

God desires and intends for us to share His joy. In fact, the Bible teaches us that God's plan for our lives includes great joy! But our heavenly Father will not compel us to be joyful. We have to accept His joy (or reject it) ourselves.

Sometimes, amid the inevitable hustle and bustle of life, we forfeit—at least for a while—God's peace. We forget and leave it behind as we struggle along the uphill climb that, for most of us, constitutes the pilgrimage through life. That pilgrimage is seldom easy, but with God as our traveling companion, we can always find strength for the journey.

So, Mom, here's a little wisdom for the road: learn to trust God, and open the door of your soul to Him. When you do, He will most certainly give you the peace and the joy He has promised.

Consider the lilies of the field. Look at the fuzz
on a baby's ear. Read in the backyard with the sun
on your face. Learn to be happy. And think of life
as a terminal illness, because, if you do, you will live it
with joy and passion, as it ought to be lived.
Anna Quindlen

Swamped by Your Possessions

Don't be obsessed with getting more material things.
Be relaxed with what you have.
Hebrews 13:5 MSG

Do you sometimes feel swamped by your possessions? Do you seem to be spending more and more time keeping track of the things you own while making mental notes of the things you intend to buy? If so, Mom, here's a word of caution: your fondness for material goods may be getting in the way of your good relationships—your relationships with the people around you and your relationship with God.

Society teaches us to honor possessions . . . God teaches us to honor Him and other people. It's as simple as that.

We must never invest too much energy in the acquisition of stuff. Earthly riches are here today and gone all too soon. Our real riches are in heaven . . . and that's where we should focus our thoughts and our energy.

When we put people before possessions in our hearts,
we are sowing seeds of enduring satisfaction.
Beverly LaHaye

Waiting Calmly for God

A patient person shows great understanding.
Proverbs 14:29 HCSB

One dictionary defines the word *patience* as "the ability to be calm, tolerant, and understanding." And for most of us, patience is a hard thing to master. Why? Because we know what we want (lots of things), and we know precisely when we want them (now—if not sooner). But the Bible teaches that we must learn to wait patiently for the things God has in store for us, even when waiting is difficult.

We live in an imperfect world inhabited by imperfect people. Sometimes we inherit trouble from others, and sometimes we create trouble for ourselves. On other occasions we see other people moving ahead in the world, and we want to move ahead with them. So we become impatient with ourselves, with our circumstances, and even with our Creator.

But do yourself this favor, Mom: be still before your heavenly Father and trust His timetable. It's the peaceful way to live.

The key to everything is patience.
You get the chicken by hatching the egg,
not by smashing it.
Ellen Glasgow

Meeting Society's Expectations

Neither exile nor homecoming is the main thing.
Cheerfully pleasing God is the main thing, and that's
what we aim to do, regardless of our conditions.
2 Corinthians 5:9 MSG

Sometimes, because we're imperfect human beings, we may become so wrapped up in meeting society's expectations that we fail to focus on God's expectations. But Mom, to do so is a mistake of major proportions—don't make it. Instead, seek God's guidance as you focus your energies on becoming the best mother you can possibly be. And when it comes to matters of conscience, seek approval not from your peers but from your Creator.

Whom will you try to please today: God or people? Your primary obligation is not to please imperfect men and women (or even children). Your obligation is to strive diligently to meet the expectations of an all-knowing and perfect God. Trust Him always. Love Him always. Praise Him always. And seek to please Him. Always.

Get ready for God to show you not only His pleasure,
but His approval.
Joni Eareckson Tada

A God Who Responds

Rejoice evermore. Pray without ceasing.
In every thing give thanks: for this is the will of God
in Christ Jesus concerning you.
1 Thessalonians 5:16–18 KJV

When we petition God, He responds. God's hand is not absent, and it is not distant. It is responsive.

On his second missionary journey, the apostle Paul started a small church in Thessalonica. A short time later he penned a letter to encourage the new believers at that church. Today, almost two thousand years later, 1 Thessalonians remains a powerful, practical guide for Christian living.

In that letter, Paul advised members of the new church to "pray without ceasing." His advice applies to people of every generation, including our own. When we weave the habit of prayer into the fabric of our days, we invite God to become a partner in every aspect of our lives.

Today, Mom, allow the responsive hand of God to guide you and help you. Pray without ceasing, and then rest assured: God is listening . . . and responding!

Prayer moves the arm that moves the world.
Annie Armstrong

God's Lessons

*He tells us everything over and over again,
a line at a time, in very simple words!*
Isaiah 28:10 NLT

When it comes to learning life's lessons, we can either do things the easy way or the hard way. The easy way can be summed up as follows: when God teaches us a lesson, we learn it—the first time. Unfortunately, too many of us (both parents and children alike) learn much more slowly than that.

When we resist God's instruction, He continues to teach us, whether we like it or not. And if we keep making the same old mistakes, God often responds by rewarding us with the same old results.

Our challenge, then, is to discern God's lessons from the experiences of everyday life. Hopefully, we learn those lessons sooner rather than later, because the sooner we do, the sooner He can move on to the next lesson . . . and the next . . .

*There are no mistakes, no coincidences;
all events are blessings given to us to learn from.*
Elisabeth Kübler-Ross

Seeking God

You will seek me and find me when you seek me
with all your heart.
Jeremiah 29:13 NIV

When we seek God with our hearts open and our prayers lifted, we need not look far: God is with us always.

Sometimes, however, in the crush of our daily duties, God may seem far away. He is not. God is everywhere we have ever been and everywhere we will ever go. He is with us night and day; He knows our thoughts and our prayers. And when we earnestly seek Him, we will find Him—because He is here, waiting patiently for us to reach out to Him.

Today, Mom, reach out to the Giver of all blessings. Turn to Him for guidance and for strength. Remember that you, a woman who has been given much, have every reason to welcome Him into your heart. And remember that no matter your circumstances, God never leaves you; He is here . . . always right here.

You will be able to trust Him only to the extent
that you know Him!
Kay Arthur

March

A Thank-You Hug for Mom

Dear Mom,

    You've always seemed to understand that a mother's attitude is contagious. Thanks for your positive attitude. When we found ourselves dwelling on the negatives of life, you helped us count our blessings instead of our troubles. Your optimism was contagious: it gave us the courage to dream . . . and the faith to believe that our dreams can come true.

Beyond the Temptations

Friend, don't go along with evil. Model the good.
The person who does good does God's work.
The person who does evil falsifies God,
doesn't know the first thing about God.
3 John 11 MSG

We are born into a world that tries its hardest to push us away from God's will. The enemy, it seems, is working 24/7 and is causing pain and heartache in more ways than ever. That's why mothers must remain watchful and strong. But the good news is this: When it comes to fighting evil, you are never alone. God is always with you, and He'll give you the power to resist temptation whenever you ask Him for strength.

In a letter, the apostle Peter offered a stern warning: "Your adversary, the devil, prowls about like a roaring lion, seeking someone to devour" (1 Peter 5:8 NASB). As a thoughtful mom, take that warning seriously and ask God to help you get beyond the temptations the enemy sets before you.

We can't stop the Adversary from whispering in our ears,
but we can refuse to listen,
and we can definitely refuse to respond.
Liz Curtis Higgs

Transformation

*His message was simple and austere,
like his desert surroundings:
"Change your life. God's kingdom is here."*
Matthew 3:2 MSG

God has the power to transform your life if you invite Him to do so. So your choice is straightforward: whether to allow the Father's transforming power to work in you and through you. It's a simple decision, but what an important decision it is!

Are you a different person because of your decision to develop a more intimate relationship with your Creator? If you can honestly answer this question with a resounding Yes! then you can be certain God will guide your steps and bless your endeavors.

God stands at the door and waits, ready to enter your heart and life; all you must do is let Him in. So today, Mom, take every step of your journey with God as your traveling companion. When you do, you'll be transformed, and you'll be blessed . . . forever.

God's work is not in buildings, but in transformed lives.
Ruth Bell Graham

Seeking Wisdom

*Does not wisdom call out? Does not understanding
raise her voice? On the heights along the way,
where the paths meet, she takes her stand.*
Proverbs 8:1–2 NIV

Do you seek wisdom for yourself and for your family? Of course you do. But as a thinking woman living in a society filled with temptations and distractions, you know that it's all too easy for parents and children alike to stray far from the source of the ultimate wisdom: God's Word.

When you commit yourself to daily study of God's Word—and when you live according to its principles—you will become wise . . . in time. But don't expect to open your Bible today and be wise tomorrow. Acquiring wisdom takes time.

Today and every day, as a way of understanding God's plan for your life, study His Word and live by it. When you do, you'll accumulate a storehouse of wisdom that will enrich your own life and the lives of your family members, your friends, and the world.

*Wise people listen to wise instruction,
especially instruction from the Word of God.*
Warren Wiersbe

Right Living

*Be holy in everything you do, just as God—who chose you
to be his children—is holy. For he himself has said,
"You must be holy because I am holy."*
1 Peter 1:15–16 NLT

When we seek to live rightly—and when we seek the companionship of people who do likewise—we'll reap the spiritual rewards God intends for us to enjoy. When you behave as a godly woman, you honor God. When you live rightly and according to God's commandments, He will bless you in ways you can't even imagine.

But in some circles, righteous living seems to have gone out of style. What a pity.

Today, as you fulfill the many responsibilities of being a mom, hold fast to what is good and associate with folks who behave themselves in like fashion. When you do, your good works will serve as a powerful example to your family and friends . . . and as a worthy offering to your Creator.

*The soul of a righteous person is nothing but a paradise,
in which, as God tells us, he takes his delight.*
Saint Teresa of Ávila

No Time Like the Present

Companions as we are in this work with you,
we beg you, please don't squander one bit
of this marvelous life God has given us.
2 Corinthians 6:1 MSG

You've heard it said on hundreds of occasions: "There's no time like the present." It's a cliché, but after all, it's true.

If you want something done, do it now. If not, tell yourself that you'll get around to it someday (knowing full well that, if you're like most folks, that someday may never actually arrive).

As a mother with lots of demands and too few hours in the day to meet them all, you have plenty of responsibilities. But not all responsibilities are created equal. So it's up to you to fulfill your most important duties (like taking care of your family) first, and finish up the less important jobs later—if and when you ever get around to them. Father's orders.

Life isn't a matter of milestones but of moments.
Rose Kennedy

The Foundations of Friendship

Putting away lying, "Let each one of you speak truth with his neighbor," for we are members of one another.
Ephesians 4:25 NKJV

Family ties and lasting friendships are built on a foundation of honesty and trust. It's been said on many occasions that honesty is the best policy. Yet it is far more important to note that honesty is God's policy.

Sometimes honesty is difficult; sometimes honesty is painful; sometimes honesty makes us feel uncomfortable. But despite these temporary feelings of discomfort, we must make honesty the hallmark of all our relationships; otherwise we invite needless suffering into our own lives and into the lives of those we love.

Sometime soon, perhaps even today, you will be tempted to bend the truth or perhaps even to break it. Resist that temptation. Truth is God's way . . . make it your way too.

How much pleasanter it would be, and how much more would be accomplished, if we did not give our word unless we intended to keep it, so that we would all know what we could depend upon.
Laura Ingalls Wilder

Louder Than Words

*Be doers of the word, and not hearers only,
deceiving yourselves.*
James 1:22 NKJV

You are a strong woman—a woman who is capable of making an enormous difference in the lives of your family and friends. And how can you make a difference? By letting your actions speak for themselves.

The old saying is both familiar and true: actions speak louder than words. So as a caring mother and a lifelong role model to your children, it's up to you to make certain your actions always speak well . . . because they do speak, both of your life and in terms of your legacy.

Sometimes you'll be tempted to talk much and do little. You'll be tempted to verbalize your beliefs rather than live by them. But it's never enough to wait idly by while others do the right thing; you, too, must act—starting now.

*There can be no happiness if the things we believe
in are different from the things we do.*
Freya Stark

Where to Take Your Troubles

*Be anxious for nothing, but in everything by prayer
and supplication, with thanksgiving,
let your requests be made known to God.*
Philippians 4:6 NKJV

Motherhood is undeniably rewarding, but it certainly does not come without challenges, frustrations, and anxieties. Sometimes, even if you're a fortunate mom living in a healthy and positive environment, you'll encounter setbacks that may leave you, at least figuratively, gasping for breath.

When you're asked to endure these life-changing personal difficulties, it's time to marshal your emotional resources: family members and friends can support you; so can your minister; members of the helping professions are waiting—and wanting—to help. But most importantly, God never leaves you, even for a moment.

Are you troubled? Share your anxieties with trusted family members, and spend a little extra time talking to God. Remember: you need never face your troubles alone . . . nor should you.

*Worry and anxiety are sand in the machinery of life;
faith is the oil.*
E. Stanley Jones

Emotional Quicksand

All bitterness, anger and wrath, insult and slander must be removed from you, along with all wickedness. And be kind and compassionate to one another, forgiving one another.
Ephesians 4:31–32 HCSB

Are you stuck in the quicksand of bitterness or regret? If so, it's time to free yourself from the mire. The world holds few if any rewards for those who remain angrily focused on the past. Still, the act of forgiveness is difficult.

Being frail, fallible, imperfect human beings, most of us are quick to anger, quick to blame, slow to forgive, and even slower to forget. Yet we know that it's best to forgive others, just as we, too, have been forgiven.

If there's even one person—including yourself—against whom you harbor bitter feelings, now is the time to forgive and move on. Bitterness and regret are not part of God's plan for you. But God won't force you to forgive others. It's a job only you can do, and the sooner you do it, the better.

You cannot live with a chip on your shoulder.
Chips make you bend your body to balance them.
And when you bend, you lose your poise, your balance,
and the chip gets into you. The real you. You get hard.
Marita Bonner

Character-Building Adversity

*We also have joy with our troubles, because we know
that these troubles produce patience. And patience
produces character, and character produces hope.*

Romans 5:3–4 NCV

The fact that we encounter adversity is not nearly as important as the way we choose to deal with it. And we must never forget that God intends for us to use our setbacks as steppingstones on the path to a better life.

When tough times come, we have a clear choice: we can begin the difficult work of tackling our troubles . . . or not. When we summon the courage to look Old Man Trouble squarely in the eye, he usually blinks. But if we refuse to address our problems, even the smallest annoyances have a way of growing into king-sized catastrophes.

We must build our lives on the Rock that cannot be shaken: we must trust in God. And then we must get on with the character-building, life-altering work of tackling our problems . . . because if we don't, who will?

*Character cannot be developed in ease and quiet.
Only through trial and suffering is the soul strengthened.*

Helen Keller

Prayer and Peace

*Don't be afraid. From the moment you decided
to humble yourself to receive understanding,
your prayer was heard, and I set out to come to you.*
Daniel 10:12 MSG

Do you seek a more peaceful life? Then lead a prayerful life. Do you have questions you can't answer? Ask for the guidance of your Father in heaven. Do you sincerely seek the gift of everlasting love and eternal life? Accept the grace of God's only Son.

When you weave the habit of prayer into the fabric of your day, you invite God to become a partner in every aspect of your life. When you consult God on a constant basis, you avail yourself of His wisdom, His strength, and His love. And because God answers prayers according to His perfect timetable, your petitions to Him—even if you don't see immediate, apparent results—will transform your family, your world, and yourself. So be good to yourself, Mom. Pray often. It's the peaceful way to live.

Prayer is a long rope with a strong hold.
Harriet Beecher Stowe

Purpose and Service

Your attitude should be the same as that of Christ Jesus:
. . . taking the very nature of a servant.
Philippians 2:5, 7 NIV

As you seek to discover God's purpose for your life, you may rest assured that His plan for you is centered on service—service to your family, to your friends, to your church, to your community, and to the world.

And yet it's not enough just to be a servant; you must also strive to be a humble servant. When you learn to serve others with genuine humility in your heart, you will build yourself up not in the eyes of people but in the eyes of God—and that's what God intends. After all, earthly glory is fleeting: here today and soon gone. But heavenly glory endures throughout eternity.

So the choice is yours: either you can lift yourself up here on earth and be humbled in heaven, or vice versa. Choose vice versa.

God has lots of folks who intend to go to work for Him
"someday." What He needs is more people
who are willing to work for Him today.
Marie T. Freeman

Life and Money

God shall supply all your need according to His riches.
Philippians 4:19 NKJV

Are you investing your money and your life in a way that makes the most of the talents God has given you? Or are you squandering your resources and your talents?

If you sincerely believe that your spending habits are pleasing to God—and if you're firmly convinced that you're using God's gifts to the best of your abilities—bravo! Keep it up. But if your spending habits are less than disciplined or your skills are not being maximized, it's time to rearrange your life and your priorities.

Do you feel overworked, underappreciated, overwhelmed, and underpaid? Are your emotions (and your credit cards) maxed out? If so, try this prescription, Mom: give yourself a double dose of discipline today . . . and you'll feel better in the morning.

Have you prayed about your resources lately?
Find out how God wants you to use your time
and your money. No matter what it costs,
forsake all that is not of God.
Kay Arthur

When You Look in the Mirror

*You made all the delicate, inner parts of my body
and knit me together in my mother's womb.
Thank you for making me so wonderfully complex!
Your workmanship is marvelous—and how well I know it.*
Psalm 139:13–14 NLT

Hey, Mom, what are you telling yourself about yourself? When you look in the mirror, are you staring back at your biggest fan or your harshest critic?

If you can learn to give yourself the benefit of the doubt—if you can learn how to have constructive conversations with the person you see in the mirror—then your self-respect will tend to take care of itself. But if you're constantly berating yourself—if you're constantly telling yourself that you can't measure up—then you'll find that self-respect is always in short supply.

You're a wonderful person just as you are. After all, you were made in the image of your wonderful Creator—and your worth is in Him. But if you're mired in the mental quicksand of overly self-critical thoughts, it's time to change your thoughts . . . and your life.

Nobody can make you feel inferior without your consent.
Eleanor Roosevelt

Your Unique Talents

There are varieties of gifts, but the same Spirit.
And there are varieties of ministries, and the same Lord.
1 Corinthians 12:4–5 NASB

God has given you an array of talents, and He has given you unique opportunities to share those talents with the world. Your Creator intends for you to use your abilities for the glory of His kingdom and in the service of His children . . . and in the service of your own children. Will you honor your heavenly Father by sharing His gifts? And will you encourage your loved ones to do the same? Hopefully, you will.

As a mother who has been given a priceless gift— your family—you must strive to make the most of your own God-given gifts. And you must do everything in your power to ensure that your children see that example and learn to do likewise. When you do, God will respond by blessing you and your family with even more gifts . . . and the cycle of blessings will continue.

We are born to make manifest the glory of God that is
within us. It is not just in some of us; it is in everyone.
As we let our own light shine, we unconsciously give
other people permission to do the same.
Nelson Mandela

Who to Trust

*The one who understands a matter finds success,
and the one who trusts in the LORD will be happy.*
Proverbs 16:20 HCSB

Here's a question for you, Mom: where will you place your trust today? Will you trust in the systems and ways of the world, or will you trust in the Word and the will of your Creator? If you aspire to do great things for God's kingdom, you will trust Him completely.

Trusting God means trusting Him in every aspect of your life. You must trust Him with your relationships. You must trust Him with your finances. You must follow His guidance. Then you can anticipate God's blessings.

When you trust your heavenly Father without reservation, you can rest assured that in His own fashion and in His own time, God will bless you in wonderful and unexpected ways. So trust Him, and then prepare yourself for the abundance and joy that will most certainly be yours through Him.

*Are you serious about wanting God's guidance
to become the person He wants you to be?
The first step is to tell God that you know you
can't manage your own life; that you need His help.*
Catherine Marshall

Staying in the Moment

*Give your entire attention to what God is doing right now,
and don't get worked up about what
may or may not happen tomorrow.*
Matthew 6:34 MSG

Because we have the ability to think, we also have the ability to worry. Even the most optimistic among us are plagued by occasional periods of discouragement and doubt. More often than not, our worries stem from our failure to focus on a priceless gift from God: the profound, precious, present moment. Instead of thanking God for the blessings of this day, we choose to fret about two more ominous days: yesterday and tomorrow. We stew about the unfairness of the past, or we agonize about the uncertainty of the future.

Perhaps you're uncertain about your future, your family, or your finances—or perhaps you're simply a worrier by nature. If so, it's time to focus less on your troubles and more on God's promises. And that's as it should be, because God is trustworthy . . . and you, Mom, are protected.

*Live in "day-tight compartments." The chief worries of life
arise from the foolish habit of looking before and after.*
William Osler

Shining Your Light

*You are the light of the world. A city on a hill cannot be
hidden. Neither do people light a lamp and put it under
a bowl. Instead they put it on its stand, and it gives light
to everyone in the house. In the same way,
let your light shine before men, that they may see
your good deeds and praise your Father in heaven.*

Matthew 5:14–16 NIV

The Bible says, "You are the light of the world."
What kind of light have you been giving off?
Hopefully, you've been a shining example for
everyone, starting with your family. Why? Because the
world needs all the light it can get, including yours!

As a mother you know that the example you
set for your family and friends is crucial. In fact,
everything you say and do serves as a testimony to
your life and your faith.

So make certain that your light—that particular
light that you and you alone can shine—is bright,
clear, visible, and pure. When you do, you'll light the
way for generations to come . . . which, by the way, is
precisely what your heavenly Father wants you to do.

*If we do not radiate the light of Christ around us,
the sense of the darkness that prevails
in the world will increase.*

Mother Teresa

Beyond the Status Quo

*You were taught to leave your old self—to stop living
the evil way you lived before. That old self becomes worse,
because people are fooled by the evil things they want to
do. But you were taught to be made new in your hearts,
to become a new person. That new person is made
to be like God—made to be truly good and holy.*
Ephesians 4:22–24 NCV

It has been said that a rut is nothing more than a grave with both ends kicked out. That's a thought worth pondering. Have you made your life an exciting adventure, or have you allowed the distractions of everyday life to rob you of a sense of God's purpose?

If you find yourself feeling as if you're stuck in a rut or in an unfortunate circumstance or in a difficult environment, abandon the status quo by making the changes your heart (and God's Word) tells you are right. After all, in God's glorious kingdom, there should be no mothers who are dejected, discouraged, or disheartened. God has a far better plan than that for you and your loved ones . . . and so should you.

*If we cannot move with change, willingly or reluctantly,
we are closer to death and further from life.*
Madeleine L'Engle

Catching the Enthusiasm

*A word spoken at the right time is like
golden apples on a silver tray.*
Proverbs 25:11 HCSB

Enthusiasm, like other human emotions, is contagious. If you associate with hope-filled, enthusiastic people, their enthusiasm will have a tendency to lift your spirits. But if you find yourself spending too much time in the company of naysayers, pessimists, or cynics, your thoughts, like theirs, will tend to be negative.

So, Mom, as you consider ways to improve your spiritual and emotional health, ask yourself whether you're associating with positive people. When you do that, you'll be availing yourself of a priceless gift: the encouragement of others.

Today look for reasons to celebrate God's countless blessings. And while you're at it, look for upbeat friends who will join with you in the celebration. You'll be better for their company, and they'll be better for yours.

*We must learn to deal with people positively
and on an individual basis.*
Mary McLeod Bethune

When the Seas Aren't Calm

[Jesus] replied, "You of little faith, why are you so afraid?"
Then he got up and rebuked the winds and the waves,
and it was completely calm.
Matthew 8:26 NIV

As every mother knows, some days are just plain difficult. We all face days when the baby is sick, the laundry is piled high, and the bills are piled even higher.

But when we find ourselves overtaken by the inevitable frustrations of life, we must catch ourselves . . . take a deep breath . . . and lift our thoughts upward. Although we're here on earth struggling to rise above the distractions of the day, we need never struggle alone. God is always with us; He is eternal and faithful.

If you find yourself enduring difficult circumstances, remember that God remains enthroned in His heaven. If you become discouraged with the direction of your day or your life, take a moment to offer your thoughts and prayers to Him. He is a God of possibility, not negativity. He will guide you through your difficulties and beyond them—beginning right now—if you ask.

To be tested is good.
The challenged life may be the best therapist.
Gail Sheehy

Impatience

Patience is better than pride.
Ecclesiastes 7:8 NLT

The rigors of parenting can test the patience of the most mild-mannered moms. From time to time even the most well-behaved children do things that worry us or confuse us or anger us. Why? Because they are children and because they're human.

As loving parents, we must be patient with our children's shortcomings (just as they, too, must be patient with ours). Sometimes the trial of being patient is the price we must pay for being responsible moms. But as our children learn and grow, making the inevitable missteps along the way, they need patient parents—and that's precisely the kind of parents we should try to be.

So do yourself and your loved ones this favor today: be patient with everyone, starting with those incredibly special little people who happen to call you Mom.

I was taught that the way of progress
is neither swift nor easy.
Marie Curie

Faith for the Future

We walk by faith, not by sight.
2 Corinthians 5:7 NKJV

When Mary McLeod Bethune was born in 1875 to parents who were former slaves, few could have guessed that she would change the face of American education. But she did. After teaching school for only five years, she founded the Daytona Normal and Industrial Institute for Negro Girls. That Florida school, now known as Bethune-Cookman College, continues its mission even today.

In the early days, Mary operated on a shoestring. What was required was faith. She once observed, "Without faith nothing is possible. With it, nothing is impossible." How right she was.

So the next time you come face to face with the illusion of impossibility, remember what Mary McLeod Bethune showed through her life's work: faith is the foundation upon which great things— schools and other miracles—are built.

Faith sees the invisible, believes the unbelievable, and receives the impossible.
Corrie ten Boom

Getting Antsy

*Go watch the ants, you lazy person. Watch what they do
and be wise. Ants have no commander, no leader or ruler,
but they store up food in the summer and gather their
supplies at harvest. How long will you lie there,
you lazy person? When will you get up from sleeping?*

Proverbs 6:6–9 NCV

The Bible instructs us that we can learn an important lesson from a surprising source: ants. Ants are among nature's most industrious creatures. They do their work without supervision and without hesitation. We should do likewise.

God's Word is clear: We are instructed to work diligently and faithfully. We're told that the fields are ripe for the harvest, that the workers are few, and that the importance of our work is profound. Let us labor, then, without hesitation and without complaint. Nighttime is coming, when we won't be able to work. But until it does, let's honor our heavenly Father with grateful hearts and willing hands.

*The role of mother is probably
the most important career a woman can have.*

Janet Mary Riley

God's Comfort

Praise be to the God and Father of our Lord Jesus Christ.
God is the Father who is full of mercy and all comfort.
He comforts us every time we have trouble,
so when others have trouble, we can comfort them
with the same comfort God gives us.
2 Corinthians 1:3–4 NCV

We live in a world that is, at times, a frightening place. It is, at times, a discouraging place. And it's a place where our losses can be so painful and so profound that it seems we will never recover. But with God's help, and with the help of encouraging family members and friends, we can be restored.

During the darker days of life, we'll be wise to remember that God is with us always and that He offers us comfort, assurance, and peace. Our part, in such times, is to accept these gifts. That sounds easy. It's not always.

But when we trust in God's promises, the world becomes a less frightening place. With His comfort and love in our hearts, we can tackle our problems with courage, determination, and faith.

Put your hand into the hand of God.
He gives the calmness and serenity of heart and soul.
Mrs. Charles E. Cowman

Embracing God's Love

We love him, because he first loved us.
1 John 4:19 KJV

Every day of your life—indeed, every moment of your life—you are embraced by God. He is always with you, Mom, and His love for you and your family is deeper and more profound than you can imagine. And now, precisely because you are a wondrous creation treasured by God, a question presents itself: what will you do in response to God's love? That decision is yours and yours alone.

But consider: When you open yourself to God's love, you'll feel differently about yourself, your neighbors, and your world. When you accept the Father's grace and share His love, you'll be blessed not just here on earth but also throughout eternity. Accept and embrace His love today.

When once we are assured that God is good,
then there can be nothing left to fear.
Hannah Whitall Smith

Whose Values?

Moderation is better than muscle,
self-control better than political power.
Proverbs 16:32 MSG

Whether you realize it or not, your life is shaped by your values. From the time your alarm clock wakes you in the morning until the moment you lay your head on the pillow at night, your actions are guided by the values you hold most dear. If you're a follower of God, those values will be shaped by the Word of God.

Society seeks to impose its set of values on us, yet these values are often contrary to God's (and thus contrary to our own best interests). And the world makes promises it simply cannot fulfill. It promises happiness, contentment, prosperity, and abundance. But genuine abundance is not a by-product of possessions or status; it's a by-product of your thoughts, your actions, and your relationship with God. The world's promises are deceptive; God's promises are unfailing. Your challenge, Mom, is to build your value system on the firm foundation of God's promises. As a mom who wants nothing but the best for herself and her family, nothing else will suffice.

First things first; second things never.
Shirley Conran

Trusting His Timing

Humble yourselves under the mighty hand of God,
that He may exalt you in due time.
1 Peter 5:6 NKJV

If you sincerely seek to be a woman of faith, then you must learn to trust God's timing. You will be sorely tempted, however, to do otherwise. As an imperfect human being, you, like the rest of us, are impatient for things to happen. But God knows best.

God has created a world that unfolds according to His timetable, not ours . . . thank goodness! We mortals would make a terrible mess of things. God does not.

His plan doesn't always unfold the way you'd like or at the time of your own choosing. But the method and timing are God's job; your task—as a caring mom who trusts in a benevolent, all-knowing Father—is to wait patiently for God to reveal Himself. And reveal Himself He will. Always. But until God's perfect plan is made known, you must walk in faith and never lose hope. And you must continue to trust Him. Always.

When we read of the great biblical leaders,
we see that it was not uncommon for God to ask them
to wait, not just a day or two, but for years,
until God was ready for them to act.
Gloria Gaither

The Self-Fulfilling Prophecy

I will hope continually and will praise You more and more.
Psalm 71:14 HCSB

The self-fulfilling prophecy is alive, well, and living at your house. If you trust God and have faith for the future, your optimistic beliefs will give you direction and motivation.

Face facts, Mom: your thoughts have the power to help lift you up or hold you down. When you acquire the habit of hopeful thinking, you will have acquired a powerful tool for improving your life. So if you find yourself falling into the spiritual traps of worry and discouragement, take stock of your thoughts. Focus them on God and listen to His voice. And make it a point to talk to encouraging friends and family members too. Finally, learn to take your worries to God and leave them there. After all, God's Word teaches us that He can overcome every difficulty. And when God makes a promise, He keeps it.

To eat bread without hope is still slowly to starve to death.
Pearl S. Buck

Kindness Now

God has chosen you and made you his holy people.
He loves you. So always do these things: Show mercy to
others, be kind, humble, gentle, and patient.
Colossians 3:12 NCV

Never underestimate the power of kindness. You never know what kind word or gesture will significantly change someone's day or week or life.

Is your home like the Old West, a place "where seldom is heard a discouraging word, and the skies are not cloudy all day"? Or is the forecast at your house slightly overcast? If your house is a place where the rule of the day is the Golden Rule, don't change a thing. Kindness starts at home . . . but it should never end there.

So today, Mom, slow down and be alert for those who need your smile, your kind words, or your helping hand. Make kindness a centerpiece of your dealings with others. They'll be blessed, and so will you.

If I am inconsiderate about the comfort of others,
or their feelings, or even their little weaknesses;
if I am careless about their little hurts and miss
opportunities to smooth their way; if I make the sweet
running of household wheels more difficult to accomplish,
then I know nothing of Calvary's love.
Amy Carmichael

Believing in Miracles

With God's power working in us, God can do much,
much more than anything we can ask or imagine.
Ephesians 3:20 NCV

Mom, do you believe in an all-powerful God who can do miraculous things in you and through you? You should. But perhaps, as you've faced the inevitable struggles of life, you have—without realizing it—placed limitations on God. To do so is a common, though profound, mistake. God's power has no limits, and He can work mighty miracles in your life if you let Him.

Do you lack a firm faith in God's power to perform miracles for you and your loved ones? If so, you're inadvertently trying to place limitations on a God who has none. Instead of doubting your heavenly Father, place yourself in His hands. Instead of doubting His power, trust it. Expect Him to work miracles, and be watchful. With God, absolutely nothing is impossible, including an amazing assortment of miracles that He stands ready, willing, and perfectly able to perform for you and yours.

Love is the divine reality that everywhere produces
and restores life. To each and every one of us,
it gives the power of working miracles if we will.
Lydia Maria Child

April

A Thank-You Hug for Mom

Dear Mom,

Thanks for your encouragement. Even when we didn't believe in ourselves, you believed in us . . . and it showed. You understand that a mother's attitude is a powerful influence on her family. If she's optimistic, her family will tend to be likewise.

Thankfully, you never gave up on us, and you never stopped believing in our abilities. Your faith eventually rubbed off on us: now, because of you, we believe in ourselves. And that, Mom, is the power of encouragement.

Being Patient with Yourself

You're blessed when you're content with just who you are—
no more, no less. That's the moment you find yourselves
proud owners of everything that can't be bought.
Matthew 5:5 MSG

Being patient with other people can be difficult. But sometimes we find it even more difficult to be patient with ourselves. We have high expectations of ourselves, and we have lofty goals. We want to accomplish things now, not later. We want to be as "perfect" as possible, and we want our lives to unfold according to our own timetables . . . not necessarily God's. But things don't always turn out as planned. Our lives are not perfect, and neither are we.

So, Mom, here's a helpful hint for dealing (happily) with your world and yourself: be patient with all people, beginning with that particular woman who stares back at you each time you gaze into the mirror. That woman is created by God . . . and she should have your respect.

Always be a first-rate version of yourself
instead of a second-rate version of someone else.
Judy Garland

Pleasing Others

Do you think I am trying to make people accept me?
No, God is the One I am trying to please.
Galatians 1:10 NCV

If you're like most people, you seek the admiration of your neighbors, your coworkers, and your family members. But the eagerness to please others should never overshadow your eagerness to please God. In every aspect of your life, pleasing your heavenly Father should come first.

Would you like a time-tested formula for successful living—a strategy that will enrich your own life and the lives of your family members? Here's one that's proven and true: seek God's approval first and other people's approval later. Does this sound too simple? Perhaps it is simple, but it's also the surest way to reap the marvelous riches that God has in store for you and yours.

Many people never receive God's best for them
because they are addicted to the approval of others.
Joyce Meyer

When Solutions Aren't Easy

*God has not given us a spirit of fearfulness,
but one of power, love, and sound judgment.*
2 Timothy 1:7 HCSB

We all sometimes face problems that defy easy solutions. If you find yourself facing a difficult decision, here's a simple formula for making the right choice: let God decide. Instead of fretting about your future, pray about it.

When you consult your heavenly Father early and often, you'll soon discover that the quiet moments you spend with God can be very helpful. Many times God will quietly lead you along a path of His choosing . . . a path that's right for you.

So the next time you arrive at one of life's inevitable crossroads, Mom, take a moment or two to bow your head and have a chat with the Ultimate Advisor. When you do, you'll never stay lost for long.

*Good and evil both increase at compound interest.
That is why the little decisions you
and I make every day are of such infinite importance.*
C. S. Lewis

Education Issues

*We are God's co-workers. You are God's field,
God's building.*
1 Corinthians 3:9 HCSB

If you're the mother of a young child, you may be struggling with one of motherhood's most difficult dilemmas: how best to educate your child. Today educational options are greater than ever—you and your child have choices that were unknown to previous generations. As you make decisions about your child's education, remember to do the following:

• Stress the importance of education. Make yours a home in which education is clearly a high priority.

• Be assertive. When it comes to educating your child, don't be satisfied to go with the flow. Stand up and be counted . . . for your kid.

When we provide our children with a firm educational foundation, we prepare them for success . . . and we help provide for generations yet unborn.

*Real education should educate us out of self
and into something far finer; into a selflessness
which links us with all humanity.*
Nancy Astor

Encouraging Others

*He comes alongside us when we go through hard times,
and before you know it, he brings us alongside someone
else who is going through hard times so that we can be
there for that person just as God was there for us.*

2 Corinthians 1:4 MSG

Do you delight in the victories of others? Hopefully so. After all, each day provides countless opportunities to encourage others and to praise their good works. When you do so, you spread seeds of joy and happiness (which, by the way, is an excellent thing to do).

Today's society has turned criticism into an art form: we have movie critics, political pundits, talk-show tantrum throwers, angry critics, urbane critics, critics, critics, and more critics. But even if criticism has become a national pastime, the regular folks you encounter on a daily basis need less criticism, not more. In fact, what they really need is encouragement, preferably in large doses.

So put a smile on your face today and keep a steady stream of encouraging words on your lips. By blessing others, you'll also bless yourself, and when you do, God smiles.

Encouragement is the oxygen of the soul.
John Maxwell

Honoring the Family

> *If a kingdom is divided against itself,*
> *that kingdom cannot stand. If a house is divided*
> *against itself, that house cannot stand.*
> Mark 3:24–25 HCSB

Mom, as you consider God's purpose for your own life, you must also consider how your plans will affect the most important people God has entrusted to your care: your family.

Even when they're separated from us by distance and time, our loved ones never really leave us. They are always in our hearts and in our prayers.

Our families are precious gifts from the Creator. We must care for our loved ones and make time for them, even when the demands of the day are great. In a world filled with countless obligations and frequent frustrations, we may be tempted to take our families and friends for granted. But God desires otherwise. He wants us to honor Him by honoring our loved ones—by giving them our support, our time, and our cooperation.

> *What can we do to promote world peace?*
> *Go home and love your family.*
>
> Mother Teresa

Your Journey Continues

I've told you these things for a purpose:
that my joy might be your joy,
and your joy wholly mature.
John 15:11 MSG

Complete spiritual maturity is never achieved in a day, or in a year, or even in a lifetime. The journey toward spiritual maturity is a process that continues, moment by moment and day by day, throughout every stage of life. Every chapter of life has its opportunities and its challenges, and if we're wise, we continue to seek God's guidance as each new stage unfolds. When we do so, we allow the Creator who made us to keep remaking us. And that's good.

If we cease to grow, either emotionally or spiritually, we do ourselves and our loved ones a profound disservice. But if we focus our thoughts and attune our hearts to the will of God, we'll make each new day another stage in the spiritual journey . . . and our Guide will be walking right beside us.

We're prone to want God to change our circumstances,
but He wants to change our character.
We think that peace comes from the outside in,
but it comes from the inside out.
Warren Wiersbe

Counting Your Blessings

I will bless them and the places surrounding my hill.
I will send down showers in season;
there will be showers of blessings.
Ezekiel 34:26 NIV

Have you counted your blessings lately? Especially as a mom, you should make thanksgiving a habit—a regular part of your daily routine. And while you're at it, it's important that you teach your children to do likewise. After all, when you pause to consider all the wonderful things you and your loved ones have been given, isn't it right and proper to say thanks?

Take time today to make a partial list of God's gifts to you: your family, your talents, your opportunities, your possessions, and the relationships that you may, on occasion, take for granted. Then, when you've listed what's probably still just a tiny portion of your blessings, offer a prayer of gratitude to the Giver of all things good. And each day, to the best of your ability, use your gifts wisely. Consider your life a thank-you note to God.

We should spend as much time in thanking God
for His benefits as we do asking Him for them.
Saint Vincent de Paul

God's Guidance

The steps of the godly are directed by the LORD.
He delights in every detail of their lives.
Psalm 37:23 NLT

God is intensely interested in each of us, and He will guide our steps if we serve Him obediently.

When we sincerely offer heartfelt prayers to our heavenly Father, He will give direction and meaning to our lives. In fact, that's what He wants to do for us. But He won't force us to follow Him. To the contrary, God has given us the free will to choose whether we'll follow Him.

Will you trust God to guide your steps, Mom? When you entrust your life to Him without reservation, God will give you the courage to face any trial, the strength to meet any challenge, and the wisdom to live in His peace. So trust Him today and seek His guidance. When you do, your next step will be the right one.

I don't doubt that the Holy Spirit guides your decisions from within when you make them with the intention of pleasing God. The error would be to think that He speaks only within, whereas in reality He speaks also through Scripture, the Church, Christian friends, and books.
C. S. Lewis

April 10

Focusing on Purpose

*Look straight ahead, and fix your eyes on what
lies before you. Mark out a straight path for your feet;
then stick to the path and stay safe. Don't get sidetracked;
keep your feet from following evil.*
Proverbs 4:25–27 NLT

Here in the real world—a world populated by kids, dogs, husbands, dirty laundry, jammed traffic, hand sanitizer, and overdue library books—it's hard to stay focused. Ours is a world filled to the brim with distractions that can seem overwhelming at times. Your challenge as a mother is to do your best to stay focused on the big picture—the plan God has for you and your family.

Because you're a busy woman, your day is not your own: you have many responsibilities that should not, indeed cannot, be disregarded. But as you go about the business of fulfilling those responsibilities, don't forget to keep in view God's overarching purpose for your life. It's a purpose that you and only you can fulfill. And the time for action is now, because tomorrow may be too late.

*I avoid looking forward or backward,
and try to keep looking upward.*
Charlotte Brontë

Specific Prayers

God answered their prayers because they trusted him.
1 Chronicles 5:20 MSG

As the old saying goes, if it's big enough to worry about, it's big enough to pray about. Yet sometimes we don't pray about the specific details of our lives. Instead, we offer general prayers that are heavy on platitudes and light on particulars.

The next time you pray, try this: be specific about the things you ask God to do. Of course, God already knows precisely what you need—He knows infinitely more about your life than even you do. But you need the experience of talking to your Creator in honest, unambiguous language.

So today, Mom, don't be vague with God. Tell Him exactly what you need. Maybe He doesn't need to go over the details, but you do.

It is not necessary for us to set forth our petitions
before God in order to make known to Him our needs
and desires, but rather that we ourselves may realize
that in these things it is necessary
to have recourse to God's assistance.
Saint Thomas Aquinas

Integrity Now

*The godly walk with integrity;
blessed are their children after them.*
Proverbs 20:7 NLT

One of the great gifts a mother can give to her child is the opportunity to witness Mom facing life's inevitable ups and downs with unwavering integrity.

Wise women understand that integrity is a crucial building block in the foundation of a well-lived life. Integrity is a precious thing—difficult to build, but easy to tear down; smart women value it and protect it at all costs.

Living a life of integrity isn't always the easiest way, but it is always the right way. And God clearly intends that it should be your way too. So today, Mom, as you teach integrity to your kids, teach it both with your words and with your actions . . . with a decided emphasis on the latter.

*If you want to be proactive in the way you live your life,
if you want to influence your life's direction,
if you want your life to exhibit the qualities
you find desirable, and if you want to live with integrity,
then you need to know what your values are,
decide to embrace them, and practice them every day.*
John Maxwell

What to Do

The lines of purpose in your lives never grow slack,
tightly tied as they are to your future in heaven,
kept taut by hope.
Colossians 1:5 MSG

W hat on earth does God intend for me to do
with my life?" It's an easy question to ask
but, for many of us, a difficult question to answer.
Why? Because God's purposes aren't always clear to
us. Sometimes we wander aimlessly in a wilderness
of our own making. And sometimes we struggle
mightily against God in an unsuccessful attempt to
find success and happiness through our own means
rather than His.

Sometimes God's direction will be clear to you;
other times His plan will seem cloudy at best. But
even on those difficult days, when you're unsure
which way to turn, never lose sight of these truths:
God created you for a reason; He has important work
for you to do; and He's waiting patiently for you to
do it.

The next step, Mom, is up to you.

How do I love God? By doing beautifully the work
I have been given to do, by doing simply that which God
entrusted to me, in whatever form it may take.
Mother Teresa

The Simple Life

A pretentious, showy life is an empty life;
a plain and simple life is a full life.
Proverbs 13:7 MSG

We live in a world where simplicity is in short supply. Think for a moment about the complexity of your everyday life, and compare it to the lives of your ancestors. Certainly, you are the beneficiary of many technological innovations, but those innovations have a price: in all likelihood, your world is highly complex.

Unless you take firm control of your time and your life, you may be overwhelmed by an ever-growing tidal wave of complexity that threatens your happiness. But your heavenly Father understands the joys of living simply, and He wants you to know those pleasures. So do yourself a favor: keep your life as simple as possible. Simplicity is genius. When you find ways to simplify your life, you'll be on the way to improving it.

Perhaps too much of everything is as bad as too little.
Edna Ferber

A Refuge in Times of Trouble

*I will sing of your strength, in the morning
I will sing of your love; for you are my fortress,
my refuge in times of trouble.*
Psalm 59:16 NIV

Mothers of every generation have experienced adversity, and the mothers of this generation are no different. But today's moms face challenges that previous generations could have scarcely imagined. Thankfully, although the world continues to change, God's love remains constant. And He remains ready to comfort you and strengthen you whenever you turn to Him.

When you encounter the inevitable challenges of modern life—the challenges of raising your children and caring for your family in a swiftly changing world—never allow yourself to become discouraged. Instead, turn your concerns over to God. When you do, you'll discover that challenges will come and challenges will go, but God stands firm and is your faithful protector—today, tomorrow, and forever.

*God will not permit any troubles to come upon us
unless He has a specific plan by which great blessing
can come out of the difficulty.*
Peter Marshall

Every Day a Celebration

The heavens declare the glory of God,
and the sky proclaims the work of His hands.
Psalm 19:1 HCSB

Every day is a custom-made gift from God. How will you receive that gift? Will you celebrate your family and your life? Will you rejoice at God's marvelous creation? And will you do your best to share your joy with others? Hopefully so . . . but sometimes when you're faced with the inevitable distractions of everyday living, you may be tempted to put off your celebration time till tomorrow. Don't do it! The dawning of every new day, including this one, is a cause to rejoice. And the best moment to accept and enjoy God's gift is the present one.

So here's the big question, Mom: will you receive and celebrate God's blessings now or put it off until later? Are you willing to give the Creator your full attention today? Hopefully so, because He deserves it. And because when you make every day a celebration of His gifts, you'll find He gives you even more to celebrate!

Every day we live is a priceless gift of God,
loaded with possibilities to learn something new,
to gain fresh insights.
Dale Evans Rogers

Prayer and Work

Each tree is known by its own fruit.
Luke 6:44 HCSB

The adage is both familiar and true: we must pray as if everything depended upon God but work as if everything depended upon us. Yet sometimes, when we're weary and discouraged, we allow our worries to sap our energy and our hope.

God has a better way. He wants us to pray for things, and He wants us to be willing to work for the things we pray for. More importantly, God intends that our work should become His work.

Are you willing to work diligently for yourself, for your family, and for your God? And are you willing to engage in work that is pleasing to your Creator? If so, you can expect your heavenly Father to bring forth a rich harvest.

And if you have concerns as you go about this work of everyday living, take those concerns to God in prayer. He will guide your steps, steady your hand, and calm your fears. And He will reward your efforts.

If there is no wind, row.
Latin Proverb

How You Worship

*"You shall worship the L*ORD *your God,
and Him only you shall serve."*
Matthew 4:10 NKJV

All of the human race is engaged in the practice of worship. Some people choose to worship God and, as a result, reap the joy He bestows on His children. Others distance themselves from God by worshiping such things as earthly possessions or personal gratification. And when they do so, they suffer.

Today, as one way of worshiping God, make every aspect of your life a cause for celebration and praise. Praise God for the blessings and opportunities He has given you. God deserves your worship, your prayers, your praise, and your thanks. And He wants you to experience the joy that will be yours when you worship Him wholeheartedly: with your prayers, with your deeds, and with your life.

*God asks that we worship Him with our concentrated
minds as well as with our wills and emotions.
A divided and scattered mind is not effective.*
Catherine Marshall

The Chains of Perfectionism

If you wait for perfect conditions,
you will never get anything done.
Ecclesiastes 11:4 NLT

Are you bound by the chains of perfectionism? If so, it's time to lighten up on yourself (and your family).

You and your loved ones should work hard, yes. You should be disciplined and always do your best. But then, when you've done all that, you should be satisfied and at peace.

Are you one of those moms who can't stand to make a mistake? Do you think you and your kids have to be "perfect" from dawn till dusk? If so, it's time to unshackle those chains! Don't be so hard on yourself and your family—nothing in this life is perfect.

In heaven we will know perfection. But here on earth, we have a few short years to wrestle with the challenges of imperfection. Yes, wrestle with them—but don't let them paralyze you until you can't accomplish or enjoy anything. Learn to accept the life God has given you with open, loving arms.

Because we are rooted and grounded in love, we can be
relaxed and at ease, knowing that our acceptance is
not based on our performance or our perfect behavior.
Joyce Meyer

Money and Character

*The one who loves money is never satisfied with money,
and whoever loves wealth is never satisfied with income.
This too is futile.*
Ecclesiastes 5:10 HCSB

Here's a scary thought: the content of your character is demonstrated in the way you choose to spend money. If you spend wisely, and if you give God His fair share, then you're doing just fine. But if you're up to your eyeballs in debt, and if "shop till you drop" is your motto, maybe it's time to retire the credit cards and reexamine your priorities.

Our society seems to be in love with money and the things money can buy. But God is not. God cares about people, not possessions, and so must we.

So today, Mom, as you think about the things money can buy—and the things it can't—don't be afraid to pray about how to allocate your resources. And make sure you're more concerned with character than cash . . . because God most certainly is.

*Money is a mirror that, strange as it sounds,
reflects our personal weaknesses
and strengths with amazing clarity.*
Dave Ramsey

Too Much TV

We must obey God rather than human authority.
Acts 5:29 NLT

The media seem sometimes to be working around the clock in an attempt to rearrange your family's priorities in ways that may not always be in your best interest. All too often, they teach your family that physical appearance is of utmost importance, that material possessions should be acquired at almost any cost, and that the world operates independently of God's laws. But guess what? Those messages are untrue.

So here's an important question, Mom: will you control what appears on your TV screen, or will you let those messages control your family? If you're willing to exercise discretion over what images you allow to come into your home, you'll be doing your clan a king-sized favor.

Today, with no further delay, take control of your family's clicker. You'll be glad you did . . . and so, in a few years, will they.

Television: chewing gum for the eyes.
Frank Lloyd Wright

When Your Faith Is Tested

But he must ask in faith without any doubting,
for the one who doubts is like the surf of the sea,
driven and tossed by the wind.

James 1:6 NASB

When the sun is shining and all is well, it's easy to have faith. But when life takes an unexpected turn for the worse, as it will from time to time, your faith will be tested. In times of trouble and doubt, God remains faithful to you—and you must put your faith in God to help you weather the storm.

Social activist Jane Addams observed, "You do not know what life means when all the difficulties are removed. It's like eating a sweet dessert the first thing in the morning." And so it is. Distress brings into relief the good things about life—and hopefully returns our focus to the God who will see us through both the good and the bad.

So the next time you spot storm clouds on the horizon, remind yourself that difficult days must come—but that each one must also come to an end. And turn to the God who will see you through.

Trials are not enemies of faith
but opportunities to reveal God's faithfulness.
Barbara Johnson

Taking Your Burdens to God

They cried out to the LORD in their trouble;
He saved them from their distress.
Psalm 107:13 HCSB

The Bible promises this: tough times are temporary but God's love is not—God's love endures forever. So what does that mean to you? Just this: From time to time, everybody faces hardships and disappointments, and so will you. But when tough times come, God always stands ready to help you and to heal you. Your task is straightforward: you must take your burdens to Him.

Whatever the size of your challenges, Mom, God is big enough to handle them. Ask for His help today, with faith and with fervor. Instead of turning things over in your mind, turn them over to God in prayer. Instead of worrying about your next decision, ask God to lead the way. Cast your burdens upon the Eternal One who cannot be shaken, and rest assured that He always hears your prayers.

Challenges make you discover things about yourself
that you never really knew.
They're what make the instrument stretch—
what make you go beyond the norm.
Cicely Tyson

When Change Is Painful

Nothing will be impossible with God.
Luke 1:37 HCSB

When life unfolds according to our wishes, or when we meet with good fortune, we greet change with open arms. That's when we find it easy to praise God for His plan. But sometimes the changes we experience are painful. When we struggle through those difficult days, as we must from time to time, we may ask ourselves, "Why me?" Usually only God knows the answer to that question . . . and usually He isn't telling. At least not yet.

Have you endured a difficult transition that has left your head spinning or your heart broken? If so, you have a choice to make: either you can cry and complain, or you can trust God and get busy fixing what's broken. The former is a formula for disaster; the latter is a strategy for a well-lived life. So, Mom, with no further delay, let the fretting cease, and let the faith . . . and the fixing . . . begin.

Revolution begins with the self, in the self.
Toni Cade Bambara

Comforting Those in Need

*Do not withhold good from those who deserve it
when it's in your power to help them.*
Proverbs 3:27 NLT

Sometimes our world is a frightening place. On occasion we sustain losses that are so profoundly tragic and life-altering that it seems we will never recover. But with God's help and with the help of loving family members and friends, we can find the strength to go on. And sometimes we can help someone else to do the same.

In times of need, God's Word is clear: we must offer comfort to those in need by sharing not only our courage but also our faith.

Do you know someone who needs a helping hand or an encouraging word? Of course you do. And the best time to extend your helping hand is now. So as you make your plans for the day and week ahead, look for somebody to help. When you do, you'll be a powerful example to your family and a beacon of God's love to others.

*So often we think that to be encouragers we have to
produce great words of wisdom when, in fact, a few simple
syllables of sympathy and an arm around the shoulder
can often provide much needed comfort.*
Florence Littauer

How to Start Your Day

Every morning he wakes me.
He teaches me to listen like a student.
The LORD God helps me learn.
Isaiah 50:4–5 NCV

Each new day is a gift from God, and wise moms spend a few quiet moments each morning thanking the Giver. Daily life is woven together with the threads of habit, and no habit is more important to our spiritual health than the discipline of daily prayer and devotion to the Creator.

When we begin each day with heads bowed and hearts lifted, we remind ourselves of God's love, His protection, and His faithfulness. And if we're wise, we align our priorities for the coming day with the teachings God has given us in His Word.

Are you seeking to change some aspect of your life? Then take time out of your hectic schedule to spend time each day with your Creator. Do you want to improve your spiritual health? Ask for God's help, and ask for it many times each day . . . starting with the first part of your day.

Ten minutes spent in Christ's company every day—
even two minutes—will make the whole day different.
Henry Drummond

Recharging Your Batteries

Your Father knows what you need before you ask Him.
Matthew 6:8 NASB

Are you a mom who could use a little extra energy? Or a lot? If so, you're not alone. Motherhood is as demanding as it is rewarding. But here's a word of advice: if you need more energy, don't make a beeline for the medicine cabinet, because you'll never find lasting strength in a pill bottle. If you're looking for power that lasts, the best place to start is with God.

Are you (or one of your family members) feeling run down from all of life's demands? If so, ask God for strength—and while you're at it, ask Him what things He wants you to take on and which things are an unnecessary drain on your energy.

In all matters, ask for God's guidance and avail yourself of God's power. You can be certain that He hears your prayers . . . and that He will answer.

We get into trouble when we think we know what to do and we stop asking God if we're doing it.
Stormie Omartian

On the Bright Side

Make me to hear joy and gladness.
Psalm 51:8 KJV

Are you an optimistic, hopeful, enthusiastic mom? Considering all your blessings, you should be. Even so, sometimes you may find yourself pulled down by the demands and worries of everyday life. If you're feeling discouraged, exhausted, or both, then it's time to take your concerns to God. When you do, He will lift your spirits and help you put things back into perspective.

Make this promise to yourself today, and keep it: vow to be a hope-filled woman. Think optimistically about your life, your career, your family, and your future. Dwell on your dreams, not your fears. Take time to celebrate God's glorious creation. And then, when you've filled your heart with hope and gladness, share your optimism with others. They'll be better for it, and so will you.

Act as if it were impossible to fail.
Dorothea Brande

The Seeds of Happiness

*If they serve Him obediently, they will end their days
in prosperity and their years in happiness.*
Job 36:11 HCSB

Her husband Daniel Custis died unexpectedly, and young Martha was left to raise her two surviving children alone. Two years later she remarried, this time to a striking young man named George—George Washington—and the former Mrs. Custis became Martha Washington, eventually America's first First Lady.

Despite the tragedies she had endured, Martha remained optimistic. She said, "We carry the seeds of happiness with us wherever we go." And she was right. Whether we will be happy in life is largely up to us—whether we choose to nurture the seeds of happiness or the seeds of bitterness.

So the next time you're feeling troubled, fearful, apathetic, or blue, remember that wherever you go, you carry within you the potential to be happy. Realizing that potential is up to you, but it's always there, so says the mother of our country. And as you're acutely aware, mother always knows best.

*Joy cannot be pursued. It comes from within.
It is a state of being. It does not depend on circumstances,
but triumphs over circumstances.*
Billy Graham

Getting Enough Sleep

Relax and rest. GOD has showered you with blessings.
Psalm 116:7 MSG

Physical exhaustion is God's way of telling us to slow down. He expects us to work hard, but our Maker also intends for us to rest. When we fail to take the rest we need, we do a disservice to ourselves and to our families—and even to God, as our ability to work for Him is diminished.

We live in a world full of attractions that tempt us to stay up late. But too much late-night TV and too little sleep is a prescription for exhaustion.

Are your physical or spiritual batteries running low? Is your energy on the wane? Are your emotions frayed? As a mother, taking care of your family also means taking care of yourself. And taking care of yourself means getting enough rest. So tonight, at a sensible hour, turn your thoughts and your prayers to God. And when you're finished, turn off the lights and go to bed!

Taking care of yourself physically really helps emotionally.
People who get a lot of sleep, who do the things
that relieve stress, can withstand a lot of stress.
Laura Bush

May

A Thank-You Hug for Mom

Dear Mom,

Thanks for listening . . . and for trying your best to understand. Sometimes you must have been frustrated by the things we said and did. But you listened anyway. And sometimes you understood us far better than we understood ourselves.

You shared your advice (which, we regret to admit, we sometimes ignored), but you also were willing to let us make our own mistakes without saying, "I told you so."

Even when our words must have seemed silly or repetitive, you kept listening. And that made all the difference.

Managing Time

Only fools idle away their time.
Proverbs 12:11 NLT

If you want to feel good about your life, then you'll need to do whatever it takes to feel good about the way you spend your time. After all, how can you expect to build a healthy sense of self-worth if you're constantly behind in your work—or if you're continually in catch-up mode?

Time is a nonrenewable resource, but sometimes we behave as if it were limitless. We squander time chasing trivial pursuits and petty diversions. But our heavenly Father beckons each of us to a higher calling. God wants us to use our time wisely, to use it in accordance with His plan for our lives. And that's what we should want too.

So today, Mom, remember that time is God's gift to you—and it's up to you, and you alone, to honor the Giver by using it wisely.

I must govern the clock, not be governed by it.
Golda Meir

Your Beliefs and Your Life

The kingdom of God is not in talk but in power.
1 Corinthians 4:20 HCSB

Our theology must be demonstrated, not by our words, but by our actions. So we must do our best to make certain that our actions are accurate reflections of our beliefs. We can proclaim those beliefs to our hearts' content, but our proclamations will mean nothing—to our children, to others, or even to ourselves—unless we accompany our words with deeds that match.

The sermons we live are far more compelling than the ones we preach. So remember this: whether you like it or not, your life is an accurate reflection of your creed. If this fact gives you cause for concern, don't bother talking about the changes you intend to make—make them. And then, Mom, when your good deeds speak for themselves—as they most certainly will—don't interrupt.

Life is not a journey you want to make on autopilot.
Paula Rinehart

Coming Back and Moving On

Come back to the LORD and live!
Amos 5:6 NLT

All of us have made mistakes, and you, Mom, are no exception. But the good news is this: when you correct your mistakes (as best you can), and when you make your apologies (to people and to God), you're free to move on with your life. And that's precisely what you should do.

If you've made big-time blunders in the past, welcome to a very large club. But thankfully, you don't have to be perfect to be blessed. So if you're disappointed that you haven't been faultless, try spending more time focusing on your good qualities instead of on your faults. And if some aspect of your life is still distancing you from God, make changes now. It's never to soon—or too late—to come back to God and move on with your life.

To be human is to be fallible, but it is also to be capable of love and to be able to retain that childlike openness which enables us to go bravely into the darkness and towards that life of love and truth which will set us free.
Madeleine L'Engle

Focusing on Your Hopes

This hope we have as an anchor of the soul,
both sure and steadfast,
and which enters the Presence behind the veil.
Hebrews 6:19 NKJV

Paul Valéry observed, "We hope vaguely but dread precisely." How true. All too often we allow the worries of life to overwhelm our thoughts and cloud our vision. What's needed is clearer perspective, renewed faith, and a different focus.

When we focus on the frustrations of today or the uncertainties of tomorrow, we rob ourselves of peace in the present moment. But when we focus on God's grace, and when we trust in the ultimate wisdom of God's plan for our lives, our worries no longer tyrannize us.

Today, Mom, remember that your thoughts are powerful, so guard them accordingly. But remember also that God is infinitely greater than any of the challenges you face.

Be very careful what thoughts you put into your mind.
For good or bad, they will boomerang right back to you.
Beatryce Nivens

Solving Life's Riddles

*The wisdom from above is first pure, then peace-loving,
gentle, compliant, full of mercy and good fruits,
without favoritism and hypocrisy.*
James 3:17 HCSB

Life is an exercise in problem solving. Every day we are presented with a new assortment of questions, decisions, puzzles, and challenges. Thankfully, the riddles of everyday living are not too difficult to solve if we look for answers in the right places. When we have questions, we should consult God's Word; we should trust the counsel of God-fearing friends and family members; and we should listen carefully to the conscience God has placed in each of our hearts.

Are you facing a difficult decision, Mom? If so, take your concerns to God and avail yourself of the messages and mentors He has placed along your path. When you do, God will speak to your conscience in His own way and in His own time; and when He does, you can most certainly trust the answers He gives.

*Questions allow us to grow and develop and change
in our understanding of ourselves and of God.*
Madeleine L'Engle

Your Great Expectations

When dreams come true, there is life and joy.
Proverbs 13:12 NLT

Hey, Mom, do you have great expectations for your future? Are you willing to dream big dreams for yourself and your family? Are you willing to work diligently to make those dreams come true? Hopefully so—after all, God's Word tells us that we can do all things through Him. Yet most of us, even the most devout among us, live far below our potential. We take half measures; we dream small dreams; we waste precious time and energy on the distractions of the world. But God has better plans for us.

Our Creator intends that we live faithfully, hopefully, courageously, and abundantly. He knows that we are capable of so much more than the world would have us believe. He wants us to do the things we're capable of doing; and He wants us to begin doing those things today.

The future belongs to those who believe
in the beauty of their dreams.
Eleanor Roosevelt

Countless Opportunities

I will instruct you and teach you in the way you should go;
I will counsel you and watch over you.
Psalm 32:8 NIV

Each waking moment holds the potential to think a creative thought or offer a heartfelt prayer. So even if you're a mother with too many demands and too few hours in which to meet them, don't panic. Instead, be comforted in the knowledge that when you sincerely seek to know and follow God's priorities for your life, He will lead you in marvelous and surprising ways.

Remember that this is the day God has made and that He has filled it with countless opportunities to love, to serve, and to seek His guidance. Seize those opportunities. And as a gift to yourself, to your family, and to the world, slow down and establish clear priorities that are pleasing to God. When you do, you'll gain the inner peace that is your spiritual inheritance . . . a peace that is yours for the asking.

Great opportunities often disguise themselves
in small tasks.
Rick Warren

Help with Forgiving

*I will lift up my eyes to the hills—
from whence comes my help? My help comes from
the LORD, who made heaven and earth.*
Psalm 121:1–2 NKJV

There's no doubt about it: forgiveness is difficult. Being frail, fallible, imperfect human beings, we are quick to get angry and blame but slow to forgive. Yet we are instructed to forgive others, just as we, too, have been forgiven. So even when forgiveness is difficult, we must ask God to help us move beyond the spiritual stumbling blocks of bitterness and hate.

If there's even one person, alive or dead, whom you have not forgiven, follow God's example and His will for your life and find the mercy and grace to let go of those offenses. Or maybe, Mom, you're embittered against yourself for some past mistake or shortcoming. Ask God to forgive you—He will—and then forgive yourself. Then, to the best of your ability, forget. Move on. Bitterness and regret are not part of God's plan for your life. Forgiveness is, and if you simply ask, your Father will help you find it.

Forgive those who have hurt you, including yourself.
Marie T. Freeman

When We Don't Understand Why

*Trust in the LORD with all your heart;
do not depend on your own understanding.
Seek his will in all you do, and he will direct your paths.*
Proverbs 3:5–6 NLT

When our dreams come true and our plans succeed, we find it easy to thank our Creator and to trust His divine providence. But in times of sorrow or hardship, we may find ourselves questioning God's plans for our lives.

On occasion you will confront circumstances that trouble you, even shake you to the very core of your soul. It's during these times that you must find the wisdom and courage to trust your heavenly Father despite your circumstances.

Are you a mother who seeks God's blessings for yourself and your family in tough times? Then wait patiently for God's deliverance . . . and prepare yourself for the abundance and peace that will most certainly be yours when your trial is through.

*The choice for me is to either look at all things
I have lost or the things I have. To live in fear
or to live in hope. Hope comes from knowing I have
a sovereign, loving God who is in every event in my life.*
Lisa Beamer

Everyday Thanksgiving

Our prayers for you are always spilling over into thanksgivings. We can't quit thanking God our Father and Jesus our Messiah for you!

Colossians 1:3 MSG

Sometimes life can be complicated, demanding, and busy. When the rush of life leaves us running from place to place with scarcely a moment to spare, it can be hard—we may even forget—to pause and say a word of thanks to God for all the good things we've received. But when we fail to count our blessings, we rob ourselves of the happiness, the peace, and the gratitude that should be in our hearts every day.

Today, Mom, even if you're busily engaged in life, slow down long enough to consider your many blessings. You'll be reminded that there are too many to count; but take a few moments to jot down as many blessings as you can. Then give thanks to the giver of all good things: God. His love for you is eternal, as are His gifts. And it's never too soon—or too late—to offer Him thanks.

So much has been given me, I have no time to ponder over that which has been denied.

Helen Keller

Surprising Plans

No one has ever seen this, and no one has ever heard about it. No one has ever imagined what God has prepared for those who love him.
1 Corinthians 2:9 NCV

God has big plans for your family—wonderful, surprising plans—but He won't force those plans on you. To the contrary, He has given you and your family free will, the ability to make decisions on your own. Now it's up to you to make those decisions wisely.

If you and your loved ones seek to live in accordance with God's plan for your lives, you'll associate with people who, by their words and actions, encourage your spiritual growth. You will assiduously avoid two temptations: the temptation to stray from God and the temptation to squander time. And finally, you will listen carefully, even reverently, to the voice of the Creator in your heart.

God wants to use you in unexpected, wonderful ways . . . if you'll just let Him. So let Him. When you do, you'll be surprised by the creativity and beauty of His plan.

The home you've always wanted,
the home you continue to long for with all your heart,
is the home God is preparing for you!
Anne Graham Lotz

Finding Strength

The LORD is the strength of my life.
Psalm 27:1 KJV

Have you made God the cornerstone of your life, or is He relegated to a few hours on Sunday morning? Have you genuinely allowed God to reign over every corner of your heart—and your house— or have you attempted to keep Him in a spiritual compartment? The answer to these questions will determine both the direction and the quality of your day—and your life.

God loves you, Mom, and He loves every member of your family. If you let Him fill your whole heart and life, in times of trouble He will comfort you; in times of sorrow He will dry your tears. When you feel weak or sad, God is as near as your next breath. He stands at the door of your heart and waits for you to welcome Him in and allow Him to rule. Decide today to accept the peace, strength, protection, and abundance that only God can give.

He goes before us, follows behind us, and hems us safe inside the realm of His protection.
Beth Moore

Honoring God

*Honor the LORD with your possessions,
and with the firstfruits of all your increase;
so your barns will be filled with plenty.*
Proverbs 3:9–10 NKJV

Whom will you choose to honor today? If you honor God and place Him at the center of your life, every day will be a cause for celebration. But if you fail to honor your heavenly Father, you're asking for trouble, and lots of it.

Life as a mom can be hectic. When the demands of life leave you rushing around with scarcely a moment to spare, you may not take time out to thank your Creator for the blessings He has bestowed upon you. But that's a big mistake.

Do you sincerely seek to be a worthy servant of the One who has given you eternal love and eternal life? Then honor Him for who He is and for what He has done for you. And don't just honor Him on Sunday morning. Praise Him every morning . . . starting with this one.

The greatest honor you can give Almighty God is to live gladly and joyfully because of the knowledge of His love.
Juliana of Norwich

Prayer That Changes Things (and You)

*If you believe, you will receive
whatever you ask for in prayer.*
Matthew 21:22 HCSB

Is prayer an integral part of your daily life, or is it a hit-and-miss happening? Do you "pray without ceasing," or is your prayer life an afterthought? As you consider the role prayer currently plays in your life—and the role you think it should play—remember that the quality of your spiritual life is directly related to the quality of your prayer life.

Prayer changes things—and it changes you. So, Mom, start today to build into your life the habit of daily, constant prayer. Instead of trying to figure things out yourself, ask God for His wisdom. Instead of worrying about your next decision, turn it over to God in prayer. Don't limit your prayers to mealtime and bedtime. Talk to God often, about things great and small. He's listening, and He wants to hear from you.

*Two wings are necessary to lift our souls toward God:
prayer and praise. Prayer asks. Praise accepts the answer.*
Mrs. Charles E. Cowman

The Glorious Gift of Life

Seek the LORD, and ye shall live.
Amos 5:6 KJV

This day, like every other, is filled to the brim with opportunities, challenges, and choices. But no choice you make is more important than the choice you make concerning God. Today you will either place Him at the center of your life or somewhere on the periphery. And the consequences of that choice have implications that are both temporal and eternal.

Sometimes, without our even realizing it, we gradually drift away from the One we need most. Thankfully, God never drifts away from us. He remains always present, always faithful, always loving.

As you begin this day, Mom, place God where He belongs: in your thoughts, in your prayers, in your speech, and in your heart. And then, with the Creator of the universe as your guide and companion, embrace the glorious gift of life you have today.

*I don't want to get to the end of my life
and find that I just lived the length of it.
I want to have lived the width of it as well.*
Diane Ackerman

Critical Warning

Don't pick on people, jump on their failures, criticize their faults—unless, of course, you want the same treatment. Don't condemn those who are down; that hardness can boomerang. Be easy on people; you'll find life a lot easier.
Luke 6:37 MSG

From experience we know that it's easier to criticize than to correct. And we know it's easier to find faults than solutions. Yet the urge to criticize others remains a powerful one for most of us. Our task—and what an important task it is—is to break the twin habits of negative thinking and critical speech.

Negativity is highly contagious: we give it to others who, in turn, give it back to us. But this cycle can be broken by positive thoughts, heartfelt prayers, and encouraging words.

As a mother you have a unique opportunity: to help break the chains of negativity in your home. So the next time you feel the urge to be critical or negative, think again. And keep thinking until you find something genuinely positive to contribute to your family and to your world.

See everything, overlook a great deal, correct a little.
Pope John XXIII

The Right Kind of Fear

The fear of the LORD is the beginning of knowledge,
but fools despise wisdom and discipline.

Proverbs 1:7 NIV

A re you a woman who possesses a healthy respect for God's power? Hopefully so. After all, God's Word teaches that the fear of the Lord is the beginning of knowledge.

When we "fear," or have reverence for, the Creator—and when we honor Him by following Him—we'll receive God's approval and His blessings. But when we ignore Him or refuse to follow His ways, we invite disastrous consequences. God's hand shaped the universe; it shapes our lives; and we must cultivate a sincere respect for His awesome power.

The fear of the Lord is, indeed, the beginning of knowledge. So today, Mom, as you face the realities of everyday life, remember this: until you acquire a healthy, respectful fear of God's power, your education is incomplete, and so is your faith.

The remarkable thing about fearing God is that
when you fear God, you fear nothing else, whereas
if you do not fear God, you fear everything else.

Oswald Chambers

Passion for Life

Never be lacking in zeal,
but keep your spiritual fervor, serving the Lord.
Romans 12:11 NIV

Are you passionate about your life, your loved ones, your work, and your faith? As a woman who has been touched by the loving hand of God, you should be.

As a devoted mom you have every reason to be enthusiastic about life, but sometimes the struggles of everyday living may cause you to feel decidedly unenthusiastic. If you feel that your zest for life is slowly fading away, it's time to slow down, to rest, to count your blessings, and to pray. When you feel worried or weary, pray fervently for God to renew your sense of wonder and excitement.

Life with God is a glorious adventure; revel in it. When you do, God will smile upon your work, your family, and your life.

Whatever you choose to do, you have one other obligation,
and that is to yourself. Do it with passion.
If you've not yet found your passion, keep searching.
You never know when it will find you.
Condoleezza Rice

Asking for Guidance

*He Himself often withdrew
into the wilderness and prayed.*
Luke 5:16 NKJV

Have you consistently asked God for guidance in every aspect of your life? If so, then you're continually inviting your Creator to reveal Himself in a variety of ways. As a thoughtful mother living in an uncertain world, you'll want to do no less.

Do you have questions about your future that you can't answer? Ask for the insight of your heavenly Father. Do you sincerely want to know God's purpose for your life? Then ask Him to reveal it—and keep asking Him every day.

Whatever your needs—whatever your family needs—no matter how great or small, pray about them, and never lose hope. God is waiting patiently to hear from you. Please don't have Him wait a single moment longer.

*Don't be overwhelmed . . .
take it one day and one prayer at a time.*
Stormie Omartian

Because It's the Right Thing

*Are there those among you who are truly wise
and understanding? Then they should show it by
living right and doing good things with a gentleness
that comes from wisdom.*
James 3:13 NCV

Pearl S. Buck grew up half a world away, the
daughter of missionaries to China. As an adult
she called upon her childhood experiences to help
her write a series of novels about the Chinese people.
Her stories not only made her one of the world's
most beloved authors but also helped her earn a
Nobel Prize for literature. Buck once observed, "You
cannot make yourself feel something you do not feel,
but you can make yourself do right in spite of your
feelings."

The next time you have a choice between doing
what you feel like doing and doing what you know
you should do, do the right thing. Consider it a favor
you owe yourself, Mom. Because feelings come and
go, but right is always right—and it's always right for
you.

*Every word we speak, every action we take,
has an effect on the totality of humanity.
No one can escape that privilege—or that responsibility.*
Laurie Beth Jones

Respecting Yourself

Every good gift and every perfect gift is from above,
and cometh down from the Father of lights.
James 1:17 KJV

Do you place a high value on your talents, your time, your capabilities, and your opportunities? You should. But too often moms acquire the insidious habit of devaluing their time, their work, or themselves. If you've fallen into that trap, it's time for a change. Have you unintentionally been squandering opportunities or somehow selling yourself short? Do yourself and your loved ones a favor by rethinking the way you think about yourself.

No one can seize opportunities for you, and no one can build up your confidence if you're unwilling to believe in yourself—in the gifts and abilities God has given you. So if you've been talking disrespectfully to yourself or underestimating your talents, stop. God has called you His own and given you unique and special qualities. That calls for some gratitude to your heavenly Father—and some healthy respect for yourself.

There's probably little in life that matters more than
first believing in one's ability to do something,
and then having the sheer grit, the sheer determination,
the perseverance to carry it through.
Johnetta B. Cole

Strength for Your Daily Journey

God is our refuge and strength,
a very present help in trouble.
Psalm 46:1 NKJV

Even the most inspired moms can, from time to time, find themselves running on empty. Why? Because the inevitable demands of daily life can be draining, that's why!

Are you almost too weary to lift your head? Then bow it—in prayer. Are you almost too tired to spend another moment on your feet? Then get on your knees. If you ask God to strengthen you—if you petition Him with a sincere and willing heart—He'll give you the power and the courage you need to meet any challenge.

Your search to discover God's purpose for your life isn't just about the destination; it's about the journey that unfolds day by day. And that's exactly how you should seek direction and strength from your Creator: one day at a time, each day followed by the next, without exception.

When God is our strength, it is strength indeed;
when our strength is our own, it is only weakness.
Saint Augustine

Using Your Talents

God has given gifts to each of you from his great variety
of spiritual gifts. Manage them well so that
God's generosity can flow through you.
1 Peter 4:10 NLT

Your talents, resources, and opportunities are all gifts from the Giver of all good things. And the best way to say thank you for these gifts is to use them.

Do you have a particular talent? Hone that skill and use it. Do you possess financial resources? Share them. Have you been blessed by a particular opportunity, or have you experienced unusual good fortune? Use those blessings to help others.

When you share the gifts God has given you—freely and without fanfare—you invite God to bless you more and more. So today, Mom, do yourself and the world a favor: be a faithful manager of your talents and treasures. And then prepare yourself for even greater blessings that are sure to come.

Yes, we need to acknowledge our weaknesses, to confess our sins. But if we want to be active, productive participants in the realm of God, we also need to recognize our gifts, to appreciate our strengths, to build on the abilities God has given us. We need to balance humility with confidence.

Penelope Stokes

Moving Past the Past

He is the LORD. Let him do what he thinks is best.
1 Samuel 3:18 NCV

The old saying is familiar: forgive and forget. But when we've been badly hurt, forgiveness is difficult and forgetting seems downright impossible. Since we can't forget yesterday's troubles (at least not yet), we should take the opportunity to learn from them. Yesterday has much to teach us about tomorrow. (Just remember that even while we may learn from the past, we should never live in the past.)

So, Mom, instead of trying to forget the past, try a different approach: learn to accept and learn from the past . . . but live in the present. Then you can focus your thoughts and your energies not on the struggles of yesterday but rather on the open doors God has placed before you today.

I believe that forgiveness can become a continuing cycle:
because God forgives us, we're to forgive others;
because we forgive others, God forgives us.
Scripture presents both parts of the cycle.
Shirley Dobson

Abundance, Not Anxiety

Humble yourselves under the mighty hand of God, that He may exalt you at the proper time, casting all your anxiety on Him, because He cares for you.
1 Peter 5:6–7 NASB

We live in a world that often breeds anxiety and fear. When we come face to face with tough times, we can fall prey to discouragement, doubt, or depression. But our Father in heaven has better plans for us. God has promised that we can lead lives of abundance, not anxiety. In fact, His Word instructs us to "be anxious for nothing" (Philippians 4:6 NASB). But how can we put our fears to rest? By taking those fears to God and leaving them there.

As you face the challenges of everyday living, do you find yourself becoming anxious, troubled, discouraged, or fearful? If so, turn every one of your concerns over to your heavenly Father. The same God who created the universe will comfort you if you ask Him . . . so ask Him, and trust Him. And then watch in amazement as your anxieties melt into the warmth of His loving hands and the abundance of His care.

Do not borrow trouble by dreading tomorrow.
It is the dark menace of the future
that makes cowards of us all.
Dorothea Dix

Making Time for God

Happy are those who hear the joyful call to worship,
for they will walk in the light of your presence, LORD.
Psalm 89:15 NLT

If you feel overwhelmed by too many responsibilities and too few hours in the day, you're not alone. Motherhood is so demanding that sometimes you may feel as if you have no time for yourself . . . and no time for God.

Has the fast pace of life robbed you of the peace that can and should be yours? If so, you're probably too busy for your own good, and it's high time you did something about it. Thankfully, God is always available to you; your challenge, of course, is to make yourself available to Him.

Today, as a gift to yourself, to your family, and to the world, slow down long enough to claim the inner peace that is God's gift to you. It is offered freely; it has been paid for in full; it is yours for the asking. So ask . . . and enjoy.

If we would only give, just once, the same amount of
reflection to what we want to get out of life that we give to
the question of what to do with a two week's vacation,
we would be startled at our false standards
and the aimless procession of our busy days.
Dorothy Canfield Fisher

The Gift of Cheerfulness

*A cheerful look brings joy to the heart,
and good news gives health to the bones.*
Proverbs 15:30 NIV

Cheerfulness is a gift you give to others—and to yourself. And it's only right that you should be cheerful. After all, when you pause long enough to count your blessings (starting, of course, with the folks who live in your own home), you'll soon realize you have many reasons to celebrate life—to go about your day with joy in your heart and a smile on your face.

Yet sometimes, even if you're the most upbeat mom on the block, you may be plagued by feelings of ill temper or frustration (who isn't?). But even then, don't allow negative emotions to go unchecked. Instead, catch your breath, cool your heels, recount your blessings, and try to cheer somebody up. When you do, you'll discover that good cheer is like honey: it's hard to spread it around without getting a little on yourself.

*Make each day useful and cheerful and prove
that you know the worth of time by employing it well.
Then youth will be happy, old age without regret,
and life a beautiful success.*
Louisa May Alcott

Your Powerful Example

You are the light that gives light to the world. . . .
You should be a light for other people.
Live so that they will see the good things you do
and will praise your Father in heaven.
Matthew 5:14, 16 NCV

Our children learn from the lessons we teach and the lives we live, but not necessarily in that order. As mothers we serve as unforgettable role models for our children, and even our grandchildren. They are influenced by what our lives teach them, even when we think class isn't in session.

What kind of example are you? Are you the kind of mother whose life serves as a genuine example of patience and uprightness? Are you a woman whose behavior serves as a positive role model for others? Are you the kind of mom whose actions, day in and day out, are based on kindness, faithfulness, and a sincere love for God and others? If so, you'll not only be blessed, but you'll also be a powerful force for good in a world that desperately needs positive influences such as yours.

You cannot not model. It's impossible.
People will see your example, positive or negative,
as a pattern for the way life is lived.
Stephen R. Covey

Beyond Discouragement

*He gives strength to the weary
and strengthens the powerless.*
Isaiah 40:29 HCSB

When we fail to meet the expectations of others (or, for that matter, the expectations we've set for ourselves), we may be tempted to abandon hope. Thankfully, on those cloudy days when our strength is sapped and our faith is shaken, there exists a Source from which we can draw courage and wisdom.

You live in a world where expectations can be high and demands can be overwhelming. The pressures of everyday life can make you feel stifled, so it's no surprise you can get discouraged . . . but you need not stay discouraged.

If you become disheartened by the direction of your day or your life, turn your thoughts and prayers to God, and He will respond. He'll help you count your blessings instead of your hardships. And then, with a renewed spirit of optimism and hope, you can properly thank your Father in heaven for His gifts . . . by using them.

*A quiet morning with a loving God puts the events
of the upcoming day into proper perspective.*
Janette Oke

Exercise: The Intelligent Choice

I discipline my body like an athlete,
training it to do what it should. Otherwise, I fear that
after preaching to others I myself might be disqualified.
1 Corinthians 9:27 NLT

We live in a fast-food world where unhealthy choices are convenient, inexpensive, and oh-so-tempting. And we live in a digital world filled with modern conveniences that siphon away opportunities for the physical exercise needed to maintain a healthy lifestyle. As a result, too many of us find ourselves (and our families) glued to the television, with a snack in one hand and a clicker in the other.

As adults each of us bears responsibility for the general state of our physical well-being. Some aspects of health are beyond our control: illness may strike even the most fit men and women. But for most of us, physical health is a choice: it's the result of hundreds of small decisions we make every day.

Implementing a routine of regular, sensible exercise is one way of ensuring that you've done your part to care for the body God has given you. It's the intelligent choice, so make it today.

Give at least two hours every day to exercise,
for health must not be sacrificed to learning.
A strong body makes the mind strong.
Thomas Jefferson

Quiet Confidence

The result of righteousness will be peace;
the effect of righteousness will be quiet confidence forever.
Isaiah 32:17 HCSB

The world has a way of shaking your confidence if you let it. Society sends out a steady stream of messages warning you that you're not quite good enough—that you should be thinner, wealthier, more successful, and more glamorous. But these messages are intended to sell products, not to build your self-esteem, and they're messages you're better off ignoring. After all, in the eyes of the people who really matter, you're already a fabulous success . . . you're a mom! And that means you're on a profoundly important mission from God.

Today, instead of listening to the media hype, listen to your heavenly Father. When you do, you'll discover that the Creator of the universe won't try to shake your self-confidence—on the contrary, He will empower you with a sense of quiet assurance . . . if you'll just let Him.

Believe and do what God says.
The life-changing consequences will be limitless,
and the results will be confidence and peace of mind.
Franklin Graham

June

A Thank-You Hug for Mom

Dear Mom,

Thanks for the lessons about life. By your words and your actions you have taught us about love, discipline, hope, courage, responsibility, and more.

One of life's great ironies is that there's so much to learn in so little time. That's why we value the wisdom you've shared with us. You cared enough to teach, and we won't forget.

The Liberation of Forgiveness

Those who show mercy to others are happy,
because God will show mercy to them.
Matthew 5:7 NCV

Bitterness is a form of self-punishment; forgiveness is a means of self-liberation. Bitterness focuses on the injustices of the past; forgiveness focuses on the blessings of the present and the opportunities of the future. Bitterness is an emotion that defeats you; forgiveness is a decision that empowers you. Bitterness is folly; forgiveness is wisdom.

Sometimes, amid the demands of daily life, we lose perspective. Life seems out of balance, and the pressures of everyday living seem overwhelming. What's needed is a fresh perspective, a restored sense of balance . . . and God's wisdom.

When we study the Bible, we are reminded that God's reality is the ultimate reality. And if we call upon the Lord and seek to see the world through His eyes, He will give us guidance, wisdom, perspective . . . and the liberation of forgiveness.

Give me such love for God and men as will
blot out all hatred and bitterness.
Dietrich Bonhoeffer

Healthy Habits

*Beloved, I pray that in all respects you may prosper
and be in good health, just as your soul prospers.*
3 John 2 NASB

All habits begin as small, consistent decisions that may seem insignificant at first. But before long, they gain the power to change and even define us. And if you're the mother of young children, you're not just forming habits for yourself; you're also helping to shape the habits of your kids. So it's always good to take an honest look at the habits that make up the fabric of your day.

Are you and your family members eating and exercising sensibly? Have you established healthy patterns that will improve the chances that you and your loved ones will live long, healthy lives?

Once you establish healthy habits, and when you reinforce them every day, you'll be surprised at how quickly your physical, mental, and spiritual health will begin to improve. So why not start forming those healthier habits today?

*Since behaviors become habits,
make them work with you and not against you.*
E. Stanley Jones

Home Schooling

The wise store up knowledge.
Proverbs 10:14 HCSB

Responsible parents understand the value of education. Children often do not. That's why it's up to us, as the grownups in the family, to stress its importance. In the twenty-first century, education is no mere luxury. It is a powerful tool and a shining light that helps snuff out the darkness of ignorance and poverty. And when it comes to education, your child deserves nothing but the best.

Part of a good education includes training in character building: lessons about honesty, responsibility, discipline, attitude, courtesy, dignity, self-worth, and respect for others. Certainly those lessons can and should be taught in school, but the ultimate training ground should be the home.

For grownups and kids alike, it's important to remember that school is always in session. So make a commitment to teach your child something new today and every day. And what if your child is already grown? Well, that's what grandchildren are for!

Education empowers you; it places you in a position
to verbally challenge people who are giving you
a whole lot of nonsense.
Camille Cosby

Beyond Guilt

*If we claim that we're free of sin, we're only
fooling ourselves. A claim like that is errant nonsense.
On the other hand, if we admit our sins—make
a clean breast of them—he won't let us down;
he'll be true to himself. He'll forgive our sins
and purge us of all wrongdoing.*
1 John 1:8–9 MSG

All of us have made mistakes. Sometimes our failures result from our own shortsightedness. On other occasions we're swept up in events beyond our control. Under either set of circumstances, we may experience intense feelings of guilt. But God has an answer for the guilt we feel. That answer is His forgiveness.

When we ask our heavenly Father for forgiveness, He forgives us completely and without reservation. Then we must do the difficult work of forgiving ourselves in the same way God has forgiven us.

So if you're feeling guilty, it's time for a special kind of housecleaning—a housecleaning of your mind and your heart.

*Don't be bound by your guilt or your fears any longer,
but realize that sin's penalty has already been paid
by Christ completely and fully.*
Billy Graham

A Mother's Example

*God-loyal people, living honest lives,
make it much easier for their children.*
Proverbs 20:7 MSG

A mother's example doesn't last for a day, or for a month, or for a year. It lasts for a lifetime . . . and beyond. So today, as you consider the lessons you intend to teach your kids, think carefully about the importance of being a mom whose words and actions provide a positive example for the next generation and for the generations that will follow.

Every time you serve as a worthy role model, you're giving your children—and theirs—a gift that money can't buy. And since tomorrow isn't promised, you must strive to be a positive role model today, not someday.

So be encouraged and remember, Mom, that your lessons last. And strive to make sure the lessons you choose to teach are reinforced by the life you choose to live.

*Children miss nothing in sizing up their parents.
If you are only half convinced of your beliefs,
they will quickly discern that fact. Any ethical weak spot,
any indecision on your part, will be incorporated
and then magnified in your sons and daughters.
Their faith or faithlessness will be a reflection of our own.*
James Dobson

Assessing Your Attitude

Set your minds on what is above,
not on what is on the earth.
Colossians 3:2 HCSB

Life should be a cause for celebration, but sometimes we don't feel much like celebrating. In fact, when the weight of the world (and the rigors of motherhood) bear down upon our shoulders, celebration may be the last thing on our minds . . . but it shouldn't be. As God's children—and as the mothers of our own children—we have been blessed beyond measure.

This day is a nonrenewable resource—once it's gone, it's gone forever. So celebrate the life God has given you by thinking optimistically about God, yourself, your family, your day, and your future. Give thanks to your heavenly Father, who has showered you and yours with blessings, and trust in your heart that He wants to give you many more.

If we could change our attitudes, we should not only see
life differently, but life itself would come to be different.
Life would undergo a change of appearance because
we ourselves had undergone a change of attitude.
Katherine Mansfield

When Mistakes Become Lessons

*The one who conceals his sins will not prosper,
but whoever confesses and renounces them
will find mercy.*
Proverbs 28:13 HCSB

We are imperfect people living in an imperfect world; mistakes are simply part of being here. But even though mistakes are an inevitable part of life's journey, repeated mistakes shouldn't be. When we commit those inevitable blunders, we must correct them, learn from them, and pray to God for the wisdom not to repeat them. And then, if we are successful, our mistakes become lessons and our lives become adventures. We experience growth, not stagnation.

So, Mom, the next time you experience one of life's little setbacks, start looking for the lesson God is trying to teach you. It's time to learn what needs to be learned, change what needs to be changed, and move on.

*Trying to grow up hurts. You make mistakes.
You try to learn from them, and when you don't,
it hurts even more.*
Aretha Franklin

A Mother's Heart

Let love and faithfulness never leave you; . . .
write them on the tablet of your heart.
Proverbs 3:3 NIV

Few things in life are as precious or as enduring as a mother's love. Our mothers give us life, and they care for us. They nurture us when we're sick and encourage us when we're brokenhearted. Mothers are the glue that holds together not just families but nations. A mother's love is powerful and priceless.

The familiar words of 1 Corinthians 13 remind us what love is—and how vital it is for our lives. Faith is important, of course. So is hope. But love is more important still. Christ showed His love for us on the cross, and we are called upon to return His love by sharing it. We are commanded to love one another just as Christ loved us (John 13:34). That's a tall order, but as recipients of God's love, we are obligated to follow it.

Sometimes love is easy, and sometimes love is hard. But we must love others without reservation or condition. So today, Mom, give your family the greatest gift this side of heaven: give them your love as you also spread Christ's love—by word and by example.

To love is to receive a glimpse of heaven.
Karen Sunde

Facing Difficult Days

The LORD is a shelter for the oppressed,
a refuge in times of trouble. Those who know your name
trust in you, for you, O LORD, have never
abandoned anyone who searches for you.
Psalm 9:9–10 NLT

All of us face difficult days. Sometimes even the most saintly moms can become discouraged, and you're no exception. Hard times visit every family, so now is the time to prepare yourself and your loved ones for life's inevitable darker days. What you'll need in those times is a combination of faith, wisdom, courage, and teamwork. When your family stands united and trusts God in the face of adversity, no problem is too big to tackle.

If you and your loved ones find yourselves enduring difficult circumstances, remember that here on earth, adversity is part of the journey. But remember this as well: despite life's occasional hardships, when you faithfully follow and trust your heavenly Father, the end of the story will be a happy one.

There is no chance, no destiny, no fate,
that can hinder or control the firm resolve
of a determined soul.
Ella Wheeler Wilcox

Opportunities to Encourage

Encourage each other and give each other strength.
1 Thessalonians 5:11 NCV

Here's a question, Mom, that only you can answer: during a typical day, how many opportunities do you have to encourage your family and friends? Unless you're living on a deserted island, you probably have a lot! And here's a follow-up question: how often do you take advantage of those opportunities? Hopefully, the answer to question number two is, "more often than not."

Whether you realize it or not, you're surrounded by people who need an encouraging word, a helping hand, a heartfelt prayer, a smile, a hug, or a good old-fashioned pat on the back. And every time you encourage one of these folks, you'll be doing God's will by obeying God's Word. So with no further ado, let the encouragement begin.

Correction does much, but encouragement does more.
Encouragement after censure is as the sun after a shower.
Johann Wolfgang von Goethe

Your Future in His Hands

*I know the thoughts that I think toward you,
says the L<small>ORD</small>, thoughts of peace and not of evil,
to give you a future and a hope. Then you will call upon
Me and go and pray to Me, and I will listen to you.*
Jeremiah 29:11–12 NKJV

Life is like a garden. Every day God gives us opportunities to plant seeds for the future. When we plant wisely and trust God completely, the harvest will be bountiful.

Mom, are you willing to place your future in the hands of a loving and all-knowing God? Do you trust in the ultimate goodness of His plan for your life? Will you face today's challenges with optimism and hope? You should. After all, God created you for a very important reason: His reason. And you have important work to do: His work.

So today, as you live in the present and look to the future, remember that God has an important plan for you. And while you still have time, it's up to you to believe—and act—accordingly.

*The horizon leans forward,
offering you space to place new steps of change.*
Maya Angelou

Disciplining Your Child

Fools reject their parents' correction,
but anyone who accepts correction is wise.
Proverbs 15:5 NCV

If only your young children would behave maturely and responsibly, parenting would be a breeze. But here in the real world, young people don't grow into mature adults overnight. So what's a mother to do? You should be patient, you should be loving, you should be encouraging and understanding—but you should also remember that you're your child's parent, not your child's best buddy.

Responsible parents (like you) refuse to allow undisciplined behavior to go unchecked for long. Otherwise they do a profound disservice to their children.

The psychologist William James observed, "The art of being wise is knowing what to overlook." The same can be said for the art of wise parenting. And as a thoughtful and loving mom, you will need to overlook some things . . . but not everything.

Cleaning your house while your kids are still growing
is like shoveling the walk before it stops snowing.
Phyllis Diller

Cultivating God's Gifts

I remind you to fan into flame the gift of God.
2 Timothy 1:6 NIV

All women possess special gifts and talents and will have unique opportunities; you are no exception. But your skills and opportunities are no guarantee of success; they must be cultivated and nurtured; otherwise they will go unused . . . and God's gifts to you will be squandered.

Today, Mom, accept this challenge: value the talent God has given you; nourish it, make it grow, and share it with the world. And while you're at it, do your best to help your loved ones do the same. After all, if your clan really wants to thank God for the talents and opportunities He has entrusted to you, the best way to express your gratitude to the Giver is to use wisely—even reverently—the gifts He has given you.

Give the world the best you have,
and the best will come back to you.
Madeline Bridges

Keeping Up Appearances

We justify our actions by appearances;
GOD examines our motives.
Proverbs 21:2 MSG

Although the world focuses on your outward features, God sees the authentic you. Therefore, the opinions of others should be relatively unimportant to you; however, God's view of you—His understanding of your actions, your thoughts, and your motivations—should be vitally important.

Few things in life are more futile than keeping up appearances in order to impress your friends—yet the world would have you believe otherwise. Media messages tell you that everything depends on the color of your hair, the condition of your wardrobe, the model of your car, and the size of your home. But what's important is pleasing your Father in heaven. You please Him when your intentions are pure and your actions are just. When those things are in line, Mom, you will be blessed today, tomorrow, and forever.

When the focus is turned to how one looks
as opposed to what one is, we are in trouble.
Toni Morrison

Infinite Possibilities

*We know that all things work together
for the good of those who love God:
those who are called according to His purpose.*
Romans 8:28 HCSB

God is a God of infinite possibilities. But sometimes, because of our limited faith and incomplete understanding, we wrongly assume that God cannot or will not intervene in the affairs of humanity. Such assumptions are simply wrong.

Are you afraid to ask God to do big things in your life? Is your faith threadbare and worn? If so, it's time to abandon your doubts and reclaim your faith in God's promises.

God's Word makes it clear: absolutely nothing is impossible for the Lord. And since the Bible means what it says, you can be comforted in the knowledge that the Creator of the universe can do miraculous things in your life and in the lives of your loved ones. Your challenge, Mom, is to take God at His Word and to expect the miraculous. When you do your part, He will most assuredly do His.

Think big, talk big, act big. Because we have a big God.
Kathryn Kuhlman

God's Provision

The LORD is my rock and my fortress and my deliverer;
the God of my strength, in whom I will trust.
2 Samuel 22:2–3 NKJV

As a busy mother you know from experience that life is not always easy. But as a recipient of God's grace, you also know that you are protected by a loving, heavenly Father.

In times of trouble God will comfort you; in times of sorrow He will dry your tears. When you are troubled or weak or sorrowful, God is neither distant nor disinterested. To the contrary, God is always present and always vitally engaged in the events of your life. Reach out to Him, Mom, and build your future on the Rock that cannot be shaken . . . trust in God and rely on His provisions. He can provide everything you and your family members really need . . . and far, far more.

God will never let you sink under your circumstances.
He always provides a safety net,
and His love always encircles.
Barbara Johnson

Miracles at Your House

Is anything too hard for the LORD?
Genesis 18:14 NKJV

We human beings have a strange disinclination to believe in things that are beyond our meager abilities to understand. We read of God's miraculous works in Bible times, but we tell ourselves, "That was then, and this is now." But when we do so, we make a mistake. Miracles—both great and small—happen around us all day every day, but usually we're too busy to notice. Some miracles, like the twinkling of a star or the glory of a sunset, we take for granted. Other miracles, like the healing of a terminally sick patient, we chalk up to fate or to luck. We assume, incorrectly, that God is "out there" and we are "right here." Nothing could be further from the truth.

Today, trust God—His power and His miracles. And then, Mom, just wait patiently . . . something miraculous is about to happen.

The miracles in fact are a retelling in small letters
of the very same story which is written across
the whole world in letters too large for some of us to see.
C. S. Lewis

Serving as God Desires

The greatest among you must be a servant.
But those who exalt themselves will be humbled,
and those who humble themselves will be exalted.
Matthew 23:11–12 NLT

If you genuinely seek to discover God's purpose for your life, you must ask yourself this question: "How does God want me to serve my family and my community today?"

Whatever your path, whatever your career, whatever your calling, you may be certain of this: service to others is an integral part of God's plan for your life.

Every single day of your life, including this one, God will give you opportunities to serve Him by serving His children. Welcome those opportunities with open arms. They are God's gift to you, His way of allowing you to achieve greatness in His kingdom. And of this you can be certain: God wants you to serve early and often, and He will surely reward you for your willingness to share your talents and your time with your family and the world.

Some people give time, some give money,
some their skills and connections, some literally give
their life's blood. But everyone has something to give.
Barbara Bush

What Money Buys

*The love of money is a root of all kinds of evil,
and by craving it, some have wandered away from
the faith and pierced themselves with many pains.*
1 Timothy 6:10 HCSB

Our society holds material possessions in high regard. Far too many people seem to worship money and the things it can buy. But such misplaced priorities inevitably lead to disappointments and dissatisfaction. Popular opinion to the contrary, money cannot buy happiness. Period.

Money, in and of itself, is not evil; but the worship of money leads to troublesome behavior. So today, Mom, as you prioritize matters of importance for you and yours, remember that God is almighty—the dollar is not.

When we worship God, we are blessed. But if we dare to worship "the almighty dollar," we're buying into misplaced priorities . . . and we'll be the ones to pay the price of the unfortunate results.

*If a person gets his attitude toward money straight,
it will help straighten out almost
every other area of his life.*
Billy Graham

Daily Hugs

*A merry heart doeth good like a medicine:
but a broken spirit drieth the bones.*
Proverbs 17:22 KJV

Whom can you hug today? If your kids are still living under your roof, this may be the easiest question you've ever had to answer, because your youngsters always need a hug (or two). But the hugging needn't stop with kids, husbands, and close relatives.

Today you'll probably bump into quite a few folks who would appreciate an outstretched hand, a pat on the back, or a big bear hug. And if you don't slow down to offer a kind word or a heartfelt embrace, who will?

So here's your challenge for today: find at least five people who need a hug. And then do the right thing: hug with abandon. When you do, you'll discover that although a hug costs nothing, it's worth a whole lot.

*Life is short, and we have not too much time for gardening
the hearts of those who are traveling the dark way with us.
Oh, be swift to love! Make haste to be kind.*
Henri-Frédéric Amiel

Positively Possible

*I have fought a good fight, I have finished my course,
I have kept the faith.*
2 Timothy 4:7 KJV

We live in a world of infinite possibilities. But at times we may fail to see the opportunities that surround us because we focus, instead, on the inconveniences and frustrations of everyday life. But we must beware: whenever we focus too intently on life's inevitable disappointments—and as a consequence focus too little on our blessings and opportunities—we suffer.

Are you willing to look for silver linings, not clouds? Do you believe that God has good things in store for you and yours? And are you willing to look carefully for the opportunities your Creator places along your path? If so, you're a wise mom indeed. After all, no job is too big for God.

Make no mistake: God can help you and your loved ones do things you never dreamed possible . . . your job is to let Him.

*When we reach the end of our abilities,
God's possibilities are just beginning.*
Emilie Barnes

Still Learning

How much better is it to get wisdom than gold!
and to get understanding rather to be chosen than silver!
Proverbs 16:16 KJV

Mom, here's a simple question: is your education complete? The correct answer is, of course not! Whether you're twenty-five or a hundred and five, you still have lots to learn, and that's good. The world is an exciting place for thinking people like you who continue to feed their brains a steady supply of new, good thoughts.

Education is the tool by which we come to know and appreciate the world in which we live. It's a tool that we should use for good—and a tool we should share—during every stage of life.

So if you thought your education was complete, think again. And if you think class has been dismissed, you've been misinformed. For those who are willing to learn, school is never really out. Lifetime learning is both wonderful and essential, so don't skip class!

All of life is a constant education.
Eleanor Roosevelt

Gossip = Trouble

A person who gossips ruins friendships.
Proverbs 16:28 ICB

Let's face facts: gossip is bad, and at times it can be disastrous. Furthermore, the Bible clearly instructs us that gossip is wrong. Yet we human beings are often tempted (at times we feel almost compelled) to chatter about other folks behind their backs. Why? Sometimes gossipy discussions offer us a distorted sense of superiority as we look down our collective nose at others. But we should beware: the cost of gossip always exceeds its worth.

As a concerned mother, it's up to you to make sure your home is a gossip-free zone. When you do, you'll be teaching your kids a valuable lesson, and you'll ensure that your home is a place where people are respected . . . and so are God's rules.

Keep your family from the abominable practice
of backbiting.
The Old Farmer's Almanac, 1813

Beyond the World's Wisdom

The wisdom of this world is foolishness in God's sight.
1 Corinthians 3:19 NIV

The world has its own brand of wisdom, a wisdom that often is wrong . . . and sometimes dangerous. God, on the other hand, has a different brand of wisdom, a wisdom that will never lead you astray.

Where will you place your trust today? Will you trust in the wisdom of fallible men and women, or will you place your faith in God's perfect wisdom? How you live in answer to this question will determine much about the direction of your day, the mood of your family, and the quality of your decisions.

As a loving mom you have a vested interest in making good decisions for your family. God—your heavenly Father—does too. When you talk to Him early and often, and when you live by the wisdom He gives, your decisions will be sound and your family will be blessed.

God's plan for our guidance is for us to grow gradually
in wisdom before we get to the crossroads.
Bill Hybels

Your Changing Family

I am the LORD, and I do not change.
Malachi 3:6 NLT

The world is in a state of constant change, and so is your family. Kids are growing up and moving out; loved ones are growing older and passing on; careers begin and end; and the world keeps turning. Everything around you may seem to be in a state of flux, but you can be comforted: although the world is constantly changing, God is not.

If your children seem to be growing up before your eyes, don't panic. And even if other changes in your life are unfolding at a furious pace, remember that your heavenly Father is the Rock that cannot be shaken—He never changes. So rest assured: it is precisely because God does not change that you and your family can face the transitions of life with courage for today and hope for tomorrow.

The key to change is to let go of fear.
Rosanne Cash

Knowledge and Wisdom

*Grow in grace and understanding of our Master
and Savior, Jesus Christ.
Glory to the Master, now and forever!*
2 Peter 3:18 MSG

If you wish to grow as a mother and a woman, you need both knowledge and wisdom. Knowledge is found mostly in textbooks. Wisdom, on the other hand, is found mostly in God's Word.

Knowledge is an important building block in a well-lived life, and it pays rich dividends both personally and professionally. But wisdom is even more important, because it refashions not only the mind but also the heart.

When it comes to your faith, God doesn't intend for you to stand still. He wants you to keep learning and growing every day of your life. No matter how grown-up you may be, you still have growing to do on the inside. And the more you grow, the more beautiful you'll become, especially on the inside.

*The more wisdom enters our hearts,
the more we will be able to trust our hearts
in difficult situations.*
John Eldredge

Recouping Your Losses

Blessings chase the righteous!
Proverbs 13:21 NLT

Have you ever made a serious financial blunder? If so, welcome to a very large club. Almost everyone experiences financial pressures from time to time, and you probably will too.

When you make a money mistake, how do you respond? Do you learn what needs to be learned and then move on? Or do you keep making the same mistakes over and over again? The best strategy, of course, is to learn from your misfortunes and to pray for the wisdom not to repeat them. If you do so, your mistakes will become opportunities for growth—and you'll become better at managing both your money and your life.

So here's the big question, Mom: have you used your spending slip-ups as stumbling blocks or stepping-stones? The answer may determine how quickly you gain financial security and peace of mind.

If you work hard and maintain an attitude of gratitude,
you'll find it easier to manage your finances every day.
John Maxwell

Acceptance

I have learned to be content whatever the circumstances.
Philippians 4:11 NIV

Has a tragedy left you angry at the world and disappointed with God? If so, it's time to accept the unchangeable past and to have faith in the promise of tomorrow. It's time to trust God completely, and it's time to reclaim the peace—His peace—that can and should be yours.

On occasion you and your family will be confronted with situations that are hard to live with and the reasons for which you don't understand. But God does. And He has a reason for everything He does.

God doesn't always explain Himself in ways that we, as mortals with limited insight and clouded vision, can comprehend. So instead of insisting that we understand every aspect of God's unfolding plan for our lives and our universe, we must learn to be satisfied to trust Him completely. We cannot know God's hidden plans, nor can we understand His actions. We can, however, trust Him.

Life is not always what one wants it to be, but to make the best of it, as it is, is the only way of being happy.
Jennie Jerome Churchill

Quieting the Emotional Storms

The righteous will live by his faith.
Habakkuk 2:4 NIV

Sometimes, despite our best intentions, negative feelings can rob us of the peace and spiritual abundance that should be ours. When anger or anxiety separates us from the blessings God has in store, it's time to rethink our priorities and renew our faith. We must place faith above feelings. Human emotions are highly variable, decidedly unpredictable, and often unreliable. Our emotions are like the weather, only far more fickle. So it's crucial that we learn to live by faith, not by the ups and downs of our own emotional roller coasters.

Even today, at some point, you may be gripped by a strong, negative emotion. Distrust it. Rein it in. Test it. And turn it over to God. Your emotions will inevitably change; God will not. So trust Him completely and watch your feelings slowly dissolve into your faith.

Build a little fence of trust around today;
fill each space with loving work, and therein stay.
Mary Frances Butts

Beyond Blame

*Get rid of all bitterness, rage, anger, harsh words,
and slander, as well as all types of malicious behavior.*
Ephesians 4:31 NLT

To blame others for our own problems is the height of futility. Yet blaming others is a favorite human pastime. Why? Because blaming is much easier than fixing, and criticizing others is much easier than improving ourselves. So instead of solving our problems legitimately (by doing the work required to solve them), we too often fret, blame, and criticize while doing precious little else. When we do, though, our problems—quite predictably—remain unsolved.

Have you acquired the bad habit of blaming others for problems you could or should solve yourself? If so, stop wasting your time. Instead of looking for someone to blame, look for something to fix, and then get busy fixing it. And as you consider your own situation, Mom, remember this: God has a way of helping those who help themselves, but He doesn't spend much time helping those who don't.

*The willingness to accept responsibility for one's own life
is the source from which self-respect springs.*
Joan Didion

July

A Thank-You Hug for Mom

Dear Mom,

Thanks for your care, your concern, your help, and your kindness. Even in your busiest moments, you always made time for our family. Through your words and deeds, you have taught us a lesson that will last a lifetime: the power of compassion. And we will be forever grateful.

Your Cheerful Heart

A cheerful heart is good medicine,
but a broken spirit saps a person's strength.
Proverbs 17:22 NLT

Never underestimate the power of a smile, a kind word, or a hug. In other words, never underestimate the importance of cheerfulness. The Bible teaches us that a cheerful heart is like medicine: it makes us (and the people around us) feel better. So where does cheerfulness begin? Does it begin on the outside—is it a result of our possessions or our circumstances? Or does it begin on the inside, as a result of our attitudes?

The world would like you to believe that material possessions can create happiness, but as a savvy mom, you're too wise to be taken in by that. You know lasting happiness can't be bought; it's a blessing from God that usually comes along with positive thoughts, heartfelt prayers, good deeds, and a cheerful heart . . . like yours.

Wondrous is the strength of cheerfulness.
Thomas Carlyle

When Life Is Difficult

Be strong and courageous. Do not be terrified;
do not be discouraged, for the LORD your God
will be with you wherever you go.
Joshua 1:9 NIV

This world can be a dangerous and daunting place, so even if you're the most faithful mom in town, you may still find your courage tested by the inevitable disappointments and unspoken fears that accompany life in the new millennium.

The next time you find your courage tested to the limit, remember to take your fears to God. If you call upon Him, you will be comforted. Whatever your challenge, whatever your trouble, God can help you tackle it.

So don't spend too much time fretting over yesterday's failures or tomorrow's dangers. Focus, instead, on today's opportunities . . . and rest assured that God is big enough to meet every challenge you face.

God did away with all my fear.
It was time for someone to stand up–or in my case,
sit down. So I refused to move.
Rosa Parks

Taking Time to Enjoy

How happy are those who can live in your house,
always singing your praises.
Psalm 84:4 NLT

Are you a mom who takes time each day to really enjoy life and your family? Hopefully so. After all, you are the recipient of a precious gift—the gift of life. And because God has seen fit to give you this gift, it is incumbent upon you to use it and to enjoy it. But sometimes, amid the pressures of everyday living, really enjoying life may seem almost impossible. It is not.

For most of us fun is as much a function of attitude as it is a function of environment. So whether you're standing victorious atop one of life's mountains or trudging through one of life's valleys, enjoy yourself. You can have fun today, and God wants to shower you with joy . . . so, Mom, what are you waiting for? Enjoy!

Whence comes this idea that if what we are doing is fun,
it can't be God's will? The God who made giraffes,
a baby's fingernails, a puppy's tail, a crooknecked squash,
the bobwhite's call, and a young girl's giggle,
has a sense of humor. Make no mistake about that.
Catherine Marshall

Celebrating Others

*Let us think about each other
and help each other to show love and do good deeds.*
Hebrews 10:24 NCV

Your loved ones need a regular supply of encouraging words and pats on the back. And you need the rewards God gives to enthusiastic moms who are a continual source of encouragement to their families.

Each day provides countless opportunities to encourage others and to commend their good works. When we do these things, we not only plant seeds of joy and happiness, we also follow the commands of God's Word.

Today, Mom, look for the good in others—starting with your family members. And then celebrate the good you find. When you do, you'll be a powerful force of encouragement in your corner of the world . . . and an enduring blessing to your family.

*The real art of conversation is not only to say
the right thing at the right place but to leave unsaid
the wrong thing at the tempting moment.*
Dorothy Nevill

Surviving Life's Storms

He said to them, "Why are you fearful,
O you of little faith?" Then He arose and rebuked
the winds and the sea, and there was a great calm.
Matthew 8:26 NKJV

A frightening storm rose quickly on the Sea of Galilee, and Jesus's disciples were afraid. Because of their limited faith, they feared for their lives. When they turned to Jesus, He calmed the waters . . . and He rebuked His disciples for their lack of faith.

On occasion we, like the disciples, are frightened by the storms of life. Why are we afraid? Because we, like the disciples, have imperfect faith.

When we genuinely accept God's promises as absolute truth, when we trust Him with life here on earth and with life eternal, we have little to fear. Faith in God is the antidote to worry. Faith in God is the foundation of courage and the source of power for ourselves and our families. Today let's trust God more completely and, by doing so, move beyond our fears to a place of abundance, assurance, and peace.

Stop to look fear in the face.
Eleanor Roosevelt

Finding Fulfillment

*You, O God, have tested us; You have refined us
as silver is refined. You brought us into the net;
You laid affliction on our backs. You have caused men
to ride over our heads; we went through fire and through
water; but You brought us out to rich fulfillment.*
Psalm 66:10–12 NKJV

Everywhere we turn, it seems, the world promises happiness, fulfillment, and contentment. But the contentment the world offers is fleeting and incomplete. Thankfully, the fulfillment God offers is all-encompassing and everlasting.

Sometimes, amid the daily grind, we can lose sight of the real joys of life as we wrestle with the challenges that confront us. Yet fulfillment is available to folks (like you) who seek it in proper places and in proper ways.

So, Mom, here's how to find lasting fulfillment: talk (and listen) often to your Creator, think good thoughts, do good deeds, love your family, and serve your neighbors. If you do these things, you'll be blessed—and so will the people who are fortunate enough to know and love you.

*By trying to grab fulfillment everywhere,
we find it nowhere.*
Elisabeth Elliot

Choosing Wise Role Models

*Spend time with the wise and you will become wise,
but the friends of fools will suffer.*
Proverbs 13:20 NCV

Here's a simple yet effective way to strengthen your faith: choose role models whose faith in God is strong.

When you emulate godly people, you become a more godly person yourself. That's why you should seek out mentors who, by their words and their actions, help make you a better person and a better follower of God.

Today, as a gift to yourself, select from your friends and family members a mentor whose judgment you trust. Then listen carefully to your mentor's advice and be willing to accept that advice, even if accepting it requires effort or discomfort. Consider your mentor to be God's gift to you. Thank God for that gift, and use it for the glory of His kingdom.

*God often keeps us on the path by guiding us through
the counsel of friends and trusted spiritual advisors.*
Bill Hybels

The Right to Say No

*In a race, everyone runs but only one person gets
first prize. . . . To win the contest you must deny yourselves
many things that would keep you from doing your best.*
1 Corinthians 9:24–25 TLB

OK, Mom, you know all too well how many people are making demands on your time. If you're like most women, you've got plenty of people pulling you in lots of directions—starting, of course, with your family.

Perhaps you also have additional responsibilities at work or at church. Maybe you're active in community affairs, or maybe you're involved in any number of other activities that gobble up big portions of your day. If so, be sure you know when enough is enough.

Most of us feel a lot of pressure to squeeze more and more obligations onto our daily to-do lists. But you have the right to say no when you simply don't have the time, the energy, or the desire to do the job. And if you're wise, you'll learn so say no as often as necessary for the benefit of yourself and your family.

To choose time is to save time.
Francis Bacon

Good Pressure, Bad Pressure

Don't envy evil men or desire to be with them.
Proverbs 24:1 HCSB

Our world is filled with pressures: some good, some bad. The pressures that we and our loved ones feel to follow God's will and to obey Him are positive pressures. God places them on our hearts, and He intends that we act in accordance with these feelings. But we also face different pressures, ones that are definitely not from God. When we feel pressured to do things—or even to think thoughts—that lead us away from God, we must beware.

Are you satisfied to follow the crowd, or will you follow a different path, the path set forth by your Creator? If you sincerely want to please God, you must resist any pressures society imposes on you that lure you away from your heavenly Father. Instead you'll want to conform to God's will, to His path, and to His Word.

Those who follow the crowd usually get lost in it.
Rick Warren

Beyond Jealousy

Where jealousy and selfishness are,
there will be confusion and every kind of evil.
James 3:16 NCV

Are you too wise to be consumed by feelings of jealousy? Hopefully so. After all, the Bible teaches us to love our neighbors, not to envy them. But sometimes, despite our best intentions, we fall prey to feelings of resentfulness, jealousy, bitterness, and envy. Why? Because we're human, and because we live in a world that places great importance on success and material possessions (possessions that, by the way, are unimpressive to God).

The next time you feel pangs of envy invading your thoughts, remind yourself of two things: (1) envy is not in keeping with the heart of God; and (2) God has already showered you with so many blessings (starting with your family) that as a thoughtful, thankful mother, you have no need to be envious of any other person on earth.

To cure jealousy is to see it for what it is,
a dissatisfaction with self.
Joan Didion

A Good Laugh

Clap your hands, all you nations;
shout to God with cries of joy.
Psalm 47:1 NIV

Motherhood is no laughing matter—it should be taken very seriously . . . up to a point. No mother's responsibilities should be so burdensome that she forgoes her daily quota of chuckles, snickers, and guffaws. So please don't forget to laugh.

You don't have to be a standup comedian to see the humorous side of life, and you don't have to memorize a string of one-liners in order to enjoy good clean humor. Humor tends to come naturally when you enjoy healthy relationships. Plus, you're more likely to laugh if you don't take yourself too seriously.

So today, as you go about your daily activities, approach your relationships and your life with a smile on your lips and a chuckle in your heart. After all, God created laughter for a reason . . . and Father indeed knows best. So go ahead—have a good laugh!

Laugh and the world laughs with you.
Weep, and you weep alone.
Ella Wheeler Wilcox

The Wisdom of Moderation

Don't turn your back on wisdom,
for she will protect you. Love her, and she will guard you.
Proverbs 4:6 NLT

Moderation and wisdom are traveling companions. If we're wise, we'll learn to temper our appetites, our desires, and our impulses. When we do, we are blessed, in part, because God has created a world in which temperance is rewarded and intemperance is inevitably punished.

Would you like to improve your life? Then harness your appetites and restrain your impulses. Moderation is difficult, yes; it's especially difficult in a prosperous society such as ours. But the rewards of moderation are numerous and long-lasting. Claim those rewards today.

No one can force you to rein in your appetites. The decision to live temperately (and wisely) is yours and yours alone. And so are the consequences.

Contentment has a way of quieting insatiable desires.
Mary Hunt

The Plan for Your Life

The plans of hard-working people earn a profit,
but those who act too quickly become poor.
Proverbs 21:5 NCV

Perhaps you have a clearly defined plan for the future, but even if you don't, rest assured that God does. Your heavenly Father has a definite plan for every aspect of your life. Your challenge is straightforward: to sincerely pray for God's guidance and to follow the guidance you receive.

If you're feeling burdened by the demands of everyday life, you're not alone. Life is difficult at times, and uncertain. But of this you can be sure: God has a plan for you and your family. And if you seek Him, He will communicate that plan through the Holy Spirit, His Word, and your own conscience. So listen to God's voice, and be watching for His signs. He'll send you messages every day of your life, including this one. Your job is to listen, to learn, to trust . . . and then to act.

Plan at least two hours of your day,
and live according to your plan.
Dorothea Brande

Making Peace with the Past

Do not remember the past events, pay no attention
to things of old. Look, I am about to do something new;
even now it is coming. Do you not see it? Indeed,
I will make a way in the wilderness, rivers in the desert.
Isaiah 43:18–19 HCSB

Have you made peace with your past? Or are you mired in the quicksand of regret? If so, it's time to plan your escape. How can you do that? By accepting what has been and by trusting God for what will be.

Because you're only human, you may be slow to forget yesterday's disappointments; if so, you are not alone. But if you sincerely want to focus your hopes and energies on the future, then you must find ways to accept the past, no matter how difficult it may be to do so.

So, Mom, if you have not yet made peace with the past, today is the day to declare an end to all hostilities. When you do, you can turn your thoughts to the wondrous promises of God and to the glorious future He has in store for you.

They say you should not suffer through the past.
You should be able to wear it like a loose garment,
take it off and let it drop.
Eva Jessye

Working for the Harvest

*The best thing people can do is to enjoy their work,
because that is all they have. No one can help another
person see what will happen in the future.*
Ecclesiastes 3:22 NCV

Once the season for planting is upon us, the time to plant seeds is when we make time to plant seeds. And when it comes to planting God's seeds in the soil of eternity, the only certain time we have is now. Yet because we are fallible human beings with limited vision and misplaced priorities, we may be tempted to postpone.

If we hope to reap a bountiful harvest for God, for our families, and for ourselves, we must plant now. And to do that we must defeat a dreaded human frailty: the habit of procrastination. Procrastination often results from our shortsighted attempts to postpone temporary discomfort.

A far better strategy is this: whatever "it" is, do it now. Then you can enjoy peace, knowing you won't have to worry about it later.

Not now becomes never.
Martin Luther

Your Bible and Your Family

The words of the LORD are pure words,
like silver tried in a furnace.
Psalm 12:6 NKJV

Are you sincerely seeking to discover God's will and follow it? If so, study His Word and live by it. The words of Matthew 4:4 remind us that "man shall not live by bread alone, but by every word that proceeds from the mouth of God" (NKJV). We must study the Bible and meditate upon its meaning for our lives. Otherwise we deprive ourselves of a priceless gift from our Creator.

God's Word is a one-of-a-kind treasure, and a mere passing acquaintance with the Good Book is insufficient for mothers (like you) who seek to follow God and teach their children to do likewise. Dig in today and enjoy the feast of blessing and wisdom to be found in God's Word. Neither moms nor dads nor their kids should be asked to live by bread alone.

If we neglect the Bible, we cannot expect to benefit
from the wisdom and direction that result
from knowing God's Word.
Vonette Bright

Expecting Perfection

Your beliefs about these things should be kept secret between you and God. People are happy if they can do what they think is right without feeling guilty.
Romans 14:22 NCV

Expectations, expectations, expectations! As a dues-paying citizen of the twenty-first century, you know that demands can be high and expectations even higher. The media deliver an endless stream of messages that tell you how to look, how to behave, how to eat, and how to dress. For most of us those expectations are impossible to meet; but God's are not. God doesn't expect perfection . . . and neither should you.

The difference between perfectionism and realistic expectations is the difference between a life of frustration and a life of contentment. So if you or your family members are shackled by the chains of perfectionism, it's time to ask yourselves who you're trying to impress . . . and why.

Your first responsibility is to the heavenly Father who gave you life. Then you bear a responsibility to your family. But when it comes to meeting a trend-obsessed society's unrealistic expectations . . . forget it!

Perfection consists simply in being
just what God wants us to be.
Saint Thérèse of Lisieux

Your Source of Strength

Have you not known? Have you not heard?
The everlasting God, the LORD, the Creator of the ends of
the earth, neither faints nor is weary. His understanding
is unsearchable. He gives power to the weak,
and to those who have no might He increases strength.
Isaiah 40:28–29 NKJV

When the almighty and all-powerful God tells us we can depend on Him for strength, why on earth would we not make our needs known to Him? The answer, of course, is that we have no reason to ignore the Creator and every reason to rely on Him.

You have a specific purpose for the coming day, a purpose only you can fulfill. And you can be sure God will give you the strength to fulfill that purpose if you ask Him.

So today, Mom, as you make yourself available to your tribe of high-maintenance kids (and sometimes even higher-maintenance grownups), don't try to do it alone. God is willing to help . . . you just have to be willing to let Him.

Sometimes I think spiritual and physical strength
is like manna: you get just what you need
for the day, no more.
Suzanne Dale Ezell

Quality Time versus Quantity Time

Teach us to number our days,
that we may gain a heart of wisdom.
Psalm 90:12 NKJV

No one needs to tell you that caring for your family requires time—lots of time. And you've probably heard lots of talk about quality time and quantity time. Your family needs both. So as a responsible mother, you willingly invest large quantities of your time and energy in the care and nurturing of your clan.

While caring for your family, remember to do your best to ensure that God remains squarely at the center of your household. When you do, God will bless you and yours in ways you could have scarcely imagined.

As you make plans for the day ahead, and as you think about how you're going to allocate your time, make sure you're giving your family both quality and quantity. It'll be good for them . . . and for you.

May you live all the days of your life.
Jonathan Swift

God's Truth

*A person who does not have the Spirit does not accept
the truths that come from the Spirit of God.
That person thinks they are foolish and cannot understand
them, because they can only be judged to be true by
the Spirit. The spiritual person is able to judge all things,
but no one can judge him.*
1 Corinthians 2:14–15 NCV

When God's love touches our hearts and our minds, we are confronted by a powerful force: the awesome, irresistible force of God's truth. In response to that force, we will either follow God's lead by allowing Him to guide our thoughts and deeds, or we'll resist God's calling and have to accept the consequences of our misplaced priorities.

Today, as you fulfill the responsibilities God has placed before you, ask yourself this question: "Do my thoughts and actions bear witness to the ultimate truth that God has placed in my heart, or am I allowing the pressures of life to overwhelm me?" It's a profound question that only you can answer. And it may just be one of the most important questions you ask yourself today . . . or, for that matter, any day.

*The difficult truth about truth is that it often requires us
to change our perspectives, attitudes, and rules for living.*
Susan Lenzkes

Beyond Mediocrity

By their fruits you will know them.
Matthew 7:20 NKJV

Providing for a family requires work, and lots of it. And whether or not your work carries you outside the home, your efforts have earned the gratitude of your loved ones and will receive the blessings of your heavenly Father.

It's been said that there are no shortcuts to anyplace worth going. Making the grade in today's competitive workplace is not easy. In fact, it can be difficult indeed. The same can be said for the important work that occurs within the walls of your home.

God did not create you and your family for lives of mediocrity; He created you for far greater things. But accomplishing God's work is seldom easy. What's required is determination, persistence, patience, and discipline—which is perfectly fine with God. After all, He knows you're up to the task, and He has promised to help you.

I have found in work that you only get back what you put into it, but it does come back gift-wrapped.
Dr. Joyce Brothers

When Your Conscience Speaks

*The LORD says, "I will make you wise
and show you where to go."*
Psalm 32:8 NCV

When you know that you're doing what's right, you'll feel better about yourself. Why? Because you'll hear good things from that little voice in your head called your conscience. Billy Graham once observed, "Most of us follow our conscience as we follow a wheelbarrow. We push it in front of us in the direction we want to go." To do so, of course, is a mistake. Yet all of us, on occasion, have failed to listen to (and follow) the voice God planted in our hearts, and all of us have suffered the consequences.

God gave you a conscience for good reason: to serve as an early warning system and a trusted advisor. Wise mothers listen carefully to that quiet internal voice. Be sure you can count yourself among that number; when your conscience speaks, listen and learn. In all likelihood, God is trying to get His message through. And in all likelihood, it's a message you need to hear.

*It is neither safe nor prudent to do anything
against one's conscience.*
Martin Luther

The Greatest of These

Love is patient, love is kind, and is not jealous;
love does not brag and is not arrogant, does not act
unbecomingly; it does not seek its own, is not provoked,
does not take into account a wrong suffered,
does not rejoice in unrighteousness, but rejoices
with the truth; bears all things, believes all things,
hopes all things, endures all things.
1 Corinthians 13:4–7 NASB

The words of 1 Corinthians 13 remind us of the importance of love. Faith is important, of course. So too is hope. But love is more important still.

Love, like every perfect gift in this wonderful world, begins and ends with God; but the middle part is largely up to us. During the brief time we have here on earth, God has given each of us the opportunity to become a loving person—or to choose not to be. God has given each of us the opportunity to be kind, to be courteous, to be cooperative, and to be forgiving—or to choose not to be. God has given each of us the chance to obey the Golden Rule or to make up our own rules as we go.

The choices we make have consequences. The decisions we make and the results of those decisions determine the quality of our relationships. Today, Mom, choose wisely.

The strongest evidence of love is sacrifice.
Carolyn Fry

Help to Endure

*Patient endurance is what you need now,
so you will continue to do God's will.
Then you will receive all that he has promised.*
Hebrews 10:36 NLT

OK, Mom, if you've led a perfect life with absolutely no blunders, mistakes, or flops—and if your kids have done likewise—you can skip this page. But if you're like the rest of us, you know that occasional disappointments and failures are part of life. Such setbacks are simply the price of growing up and learning about life. But even when you or your kids experience bitter disappointments, you must never lose faith.

When we encounter the inevitable difficulties of life, God stands ready to help us. God promises that He is never distant, and that He is always prepared to guide us and protect us when we ask Him to. So while we are waiting for God's plans to unfold, we can be comforted in the knowledge that our Creator can overcome any obstacle, even if we cannot. And He will help us to endure until the end.

*We ought to make some progress, however little,
every day, and show some increase of fervor.
We ought to act as if we were at war—as, indeed,
we are—and never relax until we have won the victory.*
Saint Teresa of Ávila

Fully Grown

The Message bears fruit and gets larger and stronger,
just as it has in you. From the very first day you heard
and recognized the truth of what God is doing,
you've been hungry for more.
Colossians 1:6 MSG

When will you be "fully grown" spiritually? Hopefully never—or at least not until you arrive in heaven! As a woman living here on planet Earth, you're never "fully grown"; you always have the potential to keep growing.

In the quiet moments when you open your heart to God, the One who made you keeps remaking you. He gives you direction, perspective, wisdom, and courage.

Would you like a time-tested formula for spiritual growth? Here it is: keep studying God's Word, keep praying (and listening for answers), and keep trying to live in the center of God's will. When you do, you'll never stay stuck for long. You will, instead, keep growing . . . and that's precisely what God wants you to do.

Often God shuts a door in our face so that
He can open the door through which He wants us to go.
Catherine Marshall

Beyond Regret

*Don't be wishing you were someplace else
or with someone else. Where you are right now
is God's place for you. Live and obey
and love and believe right there.*
1 Corinthians 7:17 MSG

Bitterness and regret can destroy you if you let them . . . so don't let them!

If you're wrapped up in bitterness and regret, you know all too well the destructive power of these emotions. How can you rid yourself of them? First, prayerfully ask God to free you from these self-defeating feelings. Then learn to catch yourself whenever thoughts of bitterness begin to attack you, and redirect your focus. Your challenge, Mom, is simply this: learn to resist negative thoughts before they hijack your emotions . . . not after.

Nineteenth-century poet Christina Rossetti had this sound advice: "Better by far you should forget and smile than you should remember and be sad." She was right—it's better to forget than regret.

*Regret over the past leads to depression in the present
and poor decisions for the future.*
Barbara Johnson

A Little Silence Every Day

Be silent before Me.
Isaiah 41:1 HCSB

For busy moms, every day is filled with tons of tasks, dozens of distractions, and seemingly countless commitments. You live among folks who are taking life at a frantic pace—members of a clamorous society—and you're not exempt from the stress and the noise. Yet the noisier your world becomes, the more you need to carve out meaningful moments for silence and meditation.

God isn't a skywriter; He doesn't spread His instructions across the morning sky for all to see. Most often God speaks in a still, quiet voice . . . a voice that can be easily drowned out by the static of the day.

So even if your appointment book is filled from cover to cover, make time for silence. Always have at least one serious chat with your Creator each day. He's waiting to hear from you . . . and you won't want to miss what He has to say.

I always begin my prayers in silence,
for it is in the silence of the heart that God speaks.
Mother Teresa

Serving Others

*Each one of us needs to look after the good of
the people around us, asking ourselves, "How can I help?"
That's exactly what Jesus did. He didn't make it easy
for himself by avoiding people's troubles,
but waded right in and helped out.*
Romans 15:2–3 MSG

We live in a world that glorifies power, prestige, fame, and money. But Jesus taught that the most esteemed men and women in His kingdom are not the self-congratulatory leaders of society but instead are the humblest of servants.

Today you may feel tempted to build yourself up in the eyes of your neighbors. Resist that temptation. Instead, serve your neighbors quietly and without fanfare. Find a need and fill it . . . humbly. Lend a helping hand . . . anonymously. Share a word of kindness . . . with quiet sincerity. As you go about your daily activities, remember that Jesus made Himself a servant, and you, as a caring mother and a responsible member of your community, should do no less.

*Try to forget yourself in service of others.
For when we think too much of ourselves and our own
interests, we easily become despondent. But when we work
for others, our efforts return to bless us.*
Sidney Powell

Defining Success

If you do not stand firm in your faith,
then you will not stand at all.
Isaiah 7:9 HCSB

How do you define success? Do you define it as the accumulation of material possessions or the adulation of your neighbors? If so, maybe you need to rethink your priorities. Genuine success has little to do with fame or fortune; it has everything to do with God's gift of love and His promise of spiritual abundance.

Today, Mom, take a few minutes to consider your definition of success. Have you been taken in by the world's idea of successful living, or have you come to understand that real success is defined not by humans but by God? Then, after you've made certain that your priorities are in order, get out there and have a really successful day!

My mother drew a distinction between achievement and
success. She said that achievement is the knowledge
that you have studied and worked hard and done the best
that is in you. Success being praised by others.
That is nice but not as important or satisfying.
Always aim for achievement and forget about success.
Helen Hayes

Each Day a Gift

Encourage one another daily, as long as it is called Today.
Hebrews 3:13 NIV

This day is a gift from God. How will you use it? Will you celebrate God's gifts and share words of encouragement and hope with all who cross your path? Will you trust in the Father and praise Him for His glorious handiwork? Your answers to these questions will play a large part in setting the tone of your day.

For thoughtful moms like you, every new day is a cause for robust celebration. So give thanks today for the gift of life and for the God who gives it. And then make this day your gift to others by giving to your loved ones—that little clan that gives meaning to your life. Use this day, which is yet another wonderful gift from the Father above, to serve your Creator, your family, and your community.

Live today fully, expressing gratitude for all you have been, all you are right now, and all you are becoming.
Melodie Beattie

Walking with God

How happy is everyone who fears the LORD,
who walks in His ways!
Psalm 128:1 HCSB

Mom, are you tired? discouraged? fearful? Want to be comforted? Take a walk with God.

Jesus called His followers to walk with Him, and He promised that He would teach them how to live freely and lightly. Are you worried or anxious? Be confident in God's power; He will never desert you. Do you see no hope for the future? Be courageous and call upon God; He will protect you and use you according to His purposes. Are you grieving? Know that God empathizes with your suffering; He will comfort you, and in time He will dry your tears. Are you confused? Listen to the quiet voice of your heavenly Father; He is not a God of confusion.

Talk with your loving Creator today. Listen to Him and follow His ways. He is steadfast, and He is your Protector . . . wherever life may lead you.

The person who walks with God
always gets to his destination.
Henrietta Mears

August

A Thank-You Hug for Mom

Dear Mom,

Every family (including ours) needs positive role models. Thanks for being one. You've taught us some of life's most important lessons, not only by your words, but also by your actions.

You weren't always perfect—nobody is—but when you did make mistakes, you corrected them, you moved on, and we learned. Because of the example you've set, you are a powerful force for good inside our home . . . and far beyond.

Wholeness

*When the woman saw that she was not hid, she came
trembling, and falling down before him, she declared unto
him before all the people for what cause she had touched
him, and how she was healed immediately.
And he said unto her, Daughter, be of good comfort:
thy faith hath made thee whole; go in peace.*
Luke 8:47–48 KJV

Until we open our hearts to God, we are never
completely whole. Until we have placed our
hearts and our lives firmly in the hands of our loving,
heavenly Father, we are incomplete. Until we discover
the peace that passes all understanding—the peace
that God promises can be ours—we long for a sense
of inner well-being that eludes us no matter how
diligently we search.

Only through God will we discover lasting peace.
We may search far and wide for worldly substitutes,
but when we seek peace apart from God, we will find
neither peace nor God.

Today, Mom, as a gift to yourself and your family,
lay claim to the peace that really matters: God's
peace.

*To be rooted is perhaps the most important
and least recognized need of the human soul.*
Simone Weil

A Passion for Life

He did it with all his heart. So he prospered.
2 Chronicles 31:21 NKJV

When people become passionate about life, great things start to happen. So here's the big question for you, Mom: are you passionate about your faith, your family, and your future? If so, you can expect others to share your enthusiasm. But if you've made the mistake of allowing pessimism and doubt to become permanent guests at your house, it's time for a heart-to-heart talk with your Father in heaven.

When you feel worried or weary, a few moments spent in quiet conversation with the Creator can calm your fears and restore your perspective. So when in doubt, talk it out . . . with God.

Are you fully engaged in life? If so, keep up the good work! But if you ever feel the passion draining, take the time to step back and refocus your thoughts, your energies, and your prayers . . . starting, of course, with your prayers.

Heat is required to forge anything.
Every great accomplishment is the story of a flaming heart
Mary Lou Retton

Finding Happiness and Abundance

Happy are those who fear the LORD.
Yes, happy are those who delight in doing
what he commands.
Psalm 112:1 NLT

Do you desire happiness, abundance, and contentment? If so, here are some things you should do: love God and rely on Him for strength; try, to the best of your abilities, to follow God's plan for your life; and spend time reading His Word. When you do these things, you'll discover that happiness goes hand in hand with godliness.

What does life have in store for you? A world full of possibilities (but it's up to you to seize them) and God's promise of abundance (but it's up to you to accept it). So, Mom, as you embark on the next phase of your life's journey, remember to celebrate the life God has given you. Your Creator has blessed you beyond measure. When you honor Him with your prayers, your words, and your deeds, happiness and spiritual abundance will be sure to follow.

Each day comes bearing its own gifts. Untie the ribbons.
Ruth Ann Schabacker

Helpful Words

Careful words make for a careful life;
careless talk may ruin everything.
Proverbs 13:3 MSG

This world can be a difficult place, a place where many of our friends and family members are troubled by the tragedies and challenges of everyday life. And since we can never be certain who might need our help, we should be careful to speak helpful words to everybody who crosses our paths.

In the book of Ephesians, Paul wrote, "Do not let any unwholesome talk come out of your mouths, but only what is helpful for building others up according to their needs, that it may benefit those who listen" (4:29 NIV). Paul reminds us that when we choose our words carefully, we can have a powerful impact on those around us.

Today, Mom, be sure to share kind words, smiles, encouragement, and hugs with your family and friends. They need the encouragement . . . and you might be surprised how much you'll be encouraged too.

Kindness in this world will do much to help others,
not only to come into the light,
but also to grow in grace day by day.
Fanny Crosby

The Lessons of Tough Times

*No discipline seems pleasant at the time, but painful.
Later on, however, it produces a harvest of righteousness
and peace for those who have been trained by it.*
Hebrews 12:11 NIV

In the midst of adversity, you may find it difficult to see the purpose of your suffering. Yet of this you can be sure: the times that try your soul are also the times that build your character. During the darker days of life, you can learn things you're unlikely to glean during sunny, happier days. Times of adversity can—and should—be times of intense spiritual and personal growth.

The next time Old Man Trouble knocks on your door, you don't have to throw him a party . . . but remember that he has lessons to teach that you don't want to miss out on. The trouble with trouble isn't just the trouble it causes; it's also the trouble we cause ourselves if we ignore the things trouble has to teach.

*The size of your burden is never
as important as the way you carry it.*
Lena Horne

The Gift of Family

*These should learn first of all to put their religion
into practice by caring for their own family.*
1 Timothy 5:4 NIV

As every mother knows, family life is a mixture of conversations, mediations, irritations, deliberations, commiserations, frustrations, negotiations, and celebrations. In other words, the life of the typical mom is incredibly varied.

Certainly, in the life of every family, there are moments of frustration and disappointment. Lots of them. But for those who are lucky enough to live in the presence of a close-knit, caring clan, the rewards far outweigh the trials.

No family is perfect, Mom, including yours. But despite the inevitable challenges and occasional hurt feelings of family life, your family is a priceless treasure. Thank God for that treasure and celebrate it today.

*The family: we are a strange little band of characters
trudging through life sharing diseases, toothpaste, coveting
one another's desserts, hiding shampoo, borrowing
money, locking each other out of rooms, loving, laughing,
defending, and trying to figure out the common thread
that bound us all together.*
Erma Bombeck

Managing Change

The wise see danger ahead and avoid it,
but fools keep going and get into trouble.
Proverbs 27:12 NCV

Without a doubt, your world is constantly changing. So today's question for you, Mom, is this: how will you manage all those changes? Will you do your best and trust God with the rest, or will you spend fruitless hours worrying about things you can't control? How you handle change has a lot to do with how your life will play out.

The best way to confront change is head on . . . and with God by your side. The same God who created the universe will see you through any change if you ask Him for help. So ask—and then serve Him with willing hands and a trusting heart. When you follow Him, you can face each new day with confidence, knowing that though the world changes moment by moment, God's love endures—unfathomable and unchanging—forever.

Life is change; growth is optional.
Karen Kaiser Clark

Trusting the Shepherd

Even though I walk through the valley of the shadow
of death, I will fear no evil, for you are with me;
your rod and your staff, they comfort me.
Psalm 23:4 NIV

In Psalm 23 David teaches us that God is like a watchful shepherd caring for His flock, a flock that includes you. You are precious in the eyes of God— you are His priceless creation, made in His image, and protected by Him. God watches over you, and you need never be afraid. But sometimes fear has a way of slipping into the minds and hearts of even the most optimistic women—and you're no exception.

As a busy mother you know that life is not always easy. But as a recipient of God's grace, you also know that you are guided and guarded by a loving heavenly Father.

Today be still and listen for the quiet assurance of God's promises. And then place your life in His hands. He is your Shepherd today and throughout eternity . . . and you can trust Him to lead you.

God loves each of us as if there were only one of us.
Saint Augustine

Finding Contentment

*Better a dry crust with peace and quiet
than a house full of feasting, with strife.*
Proverbs 17:1 NIV

Where can you find contentment? Is it a result of wealth or power or beauty or fame? Hardly. Contentment springs from a peaceful spirit, a clear conscience, and a loving heart.

Our modern world seems preoccupied with the search for happiness. We're bombarded with messages telling us that happiness depends on what we have or how we look or where we live. But these messages are false. Enduring peace is not the result of our acquisitions; it is more the result of our dispositions. If we don't find contentment within ourselves, through God, we'll never find it outside ourselves. And we'll never find it outside of God.

Thus the search for contentment is an internal and spiritual quest, an exploration of the heart, mind, and soul. You can find contentment, Mom—indeed you will find it—if you simply look in the right places.

The key to contentment is to consider.
Consider who you are and be satisfied with that.
Consider what you have and be satisfied with that.
Consider what God's doing and be satisfied with that.
Luci Swindoll

Meeting Obligations

In all the work you are doing, work the best you can.
Work as if you were doing it for the LORD, not for people.
Colossians 3:23 NCV

Nobody needs to tell you the obvious: you have lots of responsibilities—obligations to yourself, to your family, to your community, and to your God. But which of these duties should take priority? The answer can be found in the book of Matthew: "Seek first the kingdom of God and His righteousness, and all these things will be provided for you" (6:33 HCSB).

When you seek God's kingdom first and foremost, all your other obligations have a way of falling into place. When you honor God with your time, your talents, and your prayers, you'll be much more likely to count your blessings instead of your troubles.

So do yourself and your loved ones a favor: take all your duties seriously, especially your duties to God. When you do, you'll discover that pleasing your Father in heaven isn't just the right thing to do; it's also the best way to live.

Whatever it is that you intend to do with your life,
go ahead and do it today. The sun is probably
going to rise up tomorrow morning, but you may not.
Marie T. Freeman

Beyond Our Obstacles

*Even though good people may be bothered
by trouble seven times, they are never defeated.*
Proverbs 24:16 NCV

The occasional disappointments and failures of life are unavoidable. Such setbacks are simply the price we must occasionally pay for engaging with the world around us, for pursuing our goals. But even when we experience bitter disappointments, we must never lose faith.

As a mother, you know you're far from perfect. And however wonderful they are (and they are!), your children are imperfect as well. When we make mistakes, we must correct them and learn from them. And when our kids make mistakes, we must help them do likewise.

Have you or your child made a small mistake, a medium-sized mess, or a big-time blunder? If so, remember that God's love is permanent . . . but for hardworking folks (like you), failure doesn't have to be.

*You may be disappointed if you fail,
but you are doomed if you don't try.*
Beverly Sills

Finding Forgiveness Now

*Anyone who claims to live in God's light
and hates a brother or sister is still in the dark.*
1 John 2:9 MSG

Forgiveness is seldom easy, but it's always right. When we forgive those who have hurt us, we honor God by following the example He set. But when we harbor bitterness against others, we displease God—with predictably unhappy results.

Are you easily frustrated by the shortcomings of others? Are you a prisoner of bitterness or resentment? Are you living in the past when you (and your loved ones) would be much better off if you moved into the present? Perhaps you need a refresher course in the art of forgiveness.

So here's a question for you, Mom: is there somebody out there you need to forgive? If so, today is the perfect day to do yourself a favor: forgive, forget, move on. The sooner you rid your heart of bitterness, the sooner you can start filling it with more positive emotions—like love.

Forgiveness is the key to action and freedom.
Hannah Arendt

Never Distant

The LORD is with you when you are with Him.
If you seek Him, He will be found by you.
2 Chronicles 15:2 HCSB

If you're a busy mother with more obligations than you have time to count, you know all too well that the demands of life can, on occasion, seem overwhelming. Thankfully, even on the days when you feel overburdened, overworked, overstressed, and underappreciated, God never stops trying to get His message through . . . your job is to listen.

Are you discouraged, fearful, or just plain tired? If so, be comforted by the knowledge that God is with you. In whatever condition you find yourself—whether you're happy or sad, victorious or vanquished, troubled or triumphant—you can carve out moments of solitude to celebrate God's gifts and to enjoy His presence. When you do, you'll be reminded of an important truth: God is not just near, He is here. And He's ready to help you right here, right now.

God walks with us. He scoops us up in His arms or simply sits with us in silent strength until we cannot avoid the awesome recognition that yes, even now, He is here.
Gloria Gaither

How Much Love

The LORD is good, and His love is eternal;
His faithfulness endures through all generations.
Psalm 100:5 HCSB

How much does God love you and your family members? More than you can comprehend. God's love is as vast as it is timeless; it is a boundless ocean that defies human understanding.

Yet even though we cannot fully fathom God's love, we can respond to it . . . and we should.

It's a personal decision that only you can make: you must choose whether to accept God's gift. Will you ignore His love or embrace it? Will you reciprocate it or neglect it? Will you invite your heavenly Father to dwell in the center of your heart, or will you relegate Him to the outskirts of your life? The decision is yours, and so are the consequences. So choose wisely . . . and choose today.

Before anything else, above all else, beyond everything else,
God loves us. God loves us extravagantly, ridiculously,
without limit or condition. God is in love with us . . .
God yearns for us.
Roberta Bondi

God at Work

The LORD will work out his plans for my life—
for your faithful love, O LORD, endures forever.
Psalm 138:8 NLT

Whether you realize it or not, Mom, God is busily at work at your house. He has things He wants your family to do, and He has people He wants your family to help. Your mission, should you choose to accept it, is to seek God's will and to follow it, wherever it may lead.

Sometimes God's workings are obvious to us, but at other times we may be genuinely puzzled about the direction our lives should take—or are taking. In either case, we should consult our heavenly Father on a regular (spelled d-a-i-l-y) basis. And it's a good idea to consult trusted friends and family members who can help us discern God's will. When we do these things, God will make Himself known, and He will signify His approval by the blessings He bestows upon us and our loved ones.

God has no problems, only plans.
There is never panic in heaven.
Corrie ten Boom

Lighting the Fire

This is the day which the Lord has made;
let us rejoice and be glad in it.
Psalm 118:24 NASB

Hey, Mom, are you looking forward to today with a mixture of anticipation and excitement? Or are you a little less enthused than that? Hopefully, you're excited about—and thankful for—the coming day.

No one needs to remind you that some days are filled with sweetness and light, and other days . . . aren't. But even on the dark, heavy days of life, if you look carefully, you can find much to celebrate.

As a mother you have a vitally important message to share with your family: life is worth celebrating. Share that message with gusto. Your children need to see your enthusiasm, and you don't want to miss out on the rewards that will be yours when you share your joy and your wisdom with those you love.

A person's mind is not a container to be filled
but rather a fire to be kindled.
Dorothea Brande

A Smile on Your Face

A happy heart makes the face cheerful.
Proverbs 15:13 NIV

It's been a typical day. You've cared for your family, worked your fingers to the bone, rushed from Point A to Point Z, and taken barely a moment for yourself. But have you taken time to smile? If so, you're a wise woman. If not, don't forget to slow down, take a deep breath, and consider your blessings.

God makes His joy available to us, but He won't force it on us. It's up to you to claim the spiritual riches He has in store for you.

Would you like to experience the peace and the joy that God intends for you? Then accept His gifts and lay claim to His promises. Put a smile on your face that stretches all the way down to your heart. When you do, you'll discover when you smile at God, He smiles back.

*A joyful heart is like a sunshine of God's love, the hope of eternal happiness, a burning flame of God. . . .
And if we pray, we will become that sunshine of God's love—in our own home, the place where we live, and in the world at large.*
Mother Teresa

Kindness in Action

Kind people do themselves a favor,
but cruel people bring trouble on themselves.
Proverbs 11:17 NCV

Kindness is a choice. Sometimes, when we feel happy or prosperous, being kind comes naturally and easily. Other times, when we're discouraged or tired, we can scarcely summon the energy to utter a single kind word. But the Golden Rule isn't for good days only. God intends that we make the conscious choice to treat others with kindness and respect no matter what our circumstances, no matter what our emotions. And since our circumstances and our feelings may change moment by moment, kindness is a choice we must make many times each day.

But when we make the effort, when we weave the thread of kindness into the very fabric of our lives, we enrich our lives by enriching the lives of others. And everybody is better for it.

Life is a short walk from the cradle to the grave,
and it behooves us to be kind
to one another along the way.
Alice Childress

Media Messages and You

*To acquire wisdom is to love oneself;
people who cherish understanding will prosper.*
Proverbs 19:8 NLT

Sometimes it's hard to have self-respect, especially if you pay much attention to the messages the media keep pumping out. Many of those messages, which seem to pop up just about everywhere, try to tell you how you and your family should look, how you should behave, and what you should buy.

The media industry isn't interested in making you feel better about yourself—far from it. It's interested in selling products. And one of the most effective ways marketers have found to sell things is by making the audience (you) feel dissatisfied with your current situation. That's why there's a 24/7 campaign to influence your priorities.

So here's a word of warning, Mom: Don't fall prey to media messages that conflict with your Maker's message; and don't let your kids fall prey either. You and your kids are wonderful just as God made you . . . don't let anyone tell you otherwise.

*Media exist to invest our lives with
artificial perceptions and arbitrary values.*
Marshall McLuhan

At Peace

I leave you peace; my peace I give you.
I do not give it to you as the world does.
So don't let your hearts be troubled or afraid.
John 14:27 NCV

For on-the-go moms, a moment's peace can be a scarce commodity. But no matter how numerous the interruptions and demands of your day, your heavenly Father is ever-present, always ready and willing to offer solace when you seek "the peace of God, which surpasses all understanding" (Philippians 4:7 ESV).

Have you found God's peace? Or are you still rushing after an illusion—the peace and happiness the world promises but cannot deliver? Today, as a gift to yourself, to your family, and to your friends, claim the inner peace that really can be yours: God's peace. Though it's a peace you may not be able to fully comprehend, it's a peace you can still experience frequently . . . whenever you go to its Source.

We plant seeds that will flower as results in our lives,
so best to remove the weeds of anger, avarice,
envy and doubt, that peace and abundance
may manifest for all.
Dorothy Day

On a Mission

*Everything, absolutely everything, above and below,
visible and invisible, rank after rank after rank of angels—
everything got started in him and finds its purpose in him.*

Colossians 1:16 MSG

Whether you realize it or not, you are on a personal mission for God. As a mother, that mission is straightforward: honor God, raise your children in a loving home, and be a helper to those in need.

That sounds simple enough, but some days the challenges of caring for your clan may seem overwhelming. Still, you should never become discouraged. You and God, working together, can handle anything that comes your way—and the more demanding your job becomes, the more you need to avail yourself of God's power and His peace.

Every day offers countless opportunities to serve God while serving your loved ones. When you do so, your Creator will bless you in miraculous ways. That's why you should always place God where He belongs: at the center of your family and your life.

There is no influence so powerful as that of a mother.

Sarah J. Hale

Living in Our Material World

*Let us lay aside every weight and the sin
that so easily ensnares us, and run with endurance
the race that lies before us, keeping our eyes on Jesus,
the source and perfecter of our faith.*
Hebrews 12:1–2 HCSB

On the grand stage of a well-lived life, material possessions should play a rather small role. Of course, we all need the basic necessities, but once we meet those needs for ourselves and our families, the piling up of possessions often creates more problems than it solves. Our true wealth is not of this world. We're never really rich until we are rich in spirit.

Do you sometimes find yourself wrapped up in the concerns of the material world? If so, you're not the only mom in the neighborhood to struggle with finding the right balance here. Thankfully, the trap of materialism is a trap you can escape by turning your thoughts and your prayers to more important matters. When you do, you'll be less concerned with earthly goods and will begin storing up riches that will endure throughout eternity: the spiritual kind.

*I've learned to hold everything loosely
because it hurts when God pries my fingers from it.*
Corrie ten Boom

Trusting God's Answers

Trust in the LORD with all your heart;
do not depend on your own understanding.
Proverbs 3:5 NLT

God answers our prayers. What God does not do is this: He does not always answer our prayers as soon as we might like, and He does not always answer our prayers by saying yes. God isn't an order-taker, and He's not some sort of cosmic vending machine. Sometimes—even when we want something very badly—our loving, heavenly Father responds to our requests by saying no. And we must accept His answer, even if we don't understand it (or like it).

God answers prayers, Mom, not only according to our wishes but primarily according to His master plan. We cannot know that plan, but we can know the Planner . . . and we must trust His wisdom, His righteousness, and His love. He may not always do what we like, but He always does what's in our best interest.

I tell God what I want quite simply,
without any splendid turns of phrase,
and somehow He always manages to understand me.
Saint Thérèse of Lisieux

Renewal

*I will give you a new heart
and put a new spirit within you.*
Ezekiel 36:26 HCSB

God intends that His children lead joyous lives filled with spiritual abundance and supernatural peace. But sometimes, as all mothers can attest, both of those things seem far away. It is then that we must turn to God for renewal; and when we do, He will restore us.

Have you "tapped in" to the power of God, or are you muddling along in your own strength? If you feel weary, worried, fretful, or fearful, it's time to turn to a strength much greater than your own.

The Bible promises that with God all things are possible. Are you ready to turn things over to Him? If you do, you'll soon discover that the Creator of the universe stands ready and able to renew your sense of wonder, joy, and strength.

*Be still, and in the quiet moments,
listen to the voice of your heavenly Father.
His words can renew your spirit—no one knows you
and your needs like He does.*
Janet L. Weaver Smith

The Gift of Time

While it is daytime, we must continue doing
the work of the One who sent me.
Night is coming, when no one can work.
John 9:4 NCV

Every mother knows the feeling that there simply isn't enough time to do everything we want—and need—to do. That's why we must be careful about the way we choose to spend the time God has given us.

Time is a nonrenewable gift from the Creator. But sometimes we treat time as if it were not a gift at all: we may be tempted to fritter away our lives in petty diversions or trivial pursuits. But our Father in heaven beckons each of us to a higher calling.

Each waking moment holds the potential to do a good deed, to say a kind word, or to offer a heartfelt prayer. Each day is a special treasure to be savored and celebrated. Every heartbeat marks yet another opportunity to do the right thing and to give thanks to the proper Source. And because time is short, none of us has even a minute to waste.

Exhaust the little moment. Soon it dies.
Gwendolyn Brooks

Solving Problems

People who do what is right may have many problems,
but the LORD will solve them all.
Psalm 34:19 NCV

Life is a prolonged exercise in problem solving. The question is not whether we will encounter problems; the question is how we will choose to address them. When it comes to solving the problems of everyday living, even when we know precisely what needs to be done, we may be slow in doing it—especially if what needs to be done is difficult or uncomfortable for us. So we put off till tomorrow what should be done today.

The words of Psalm 34 remind us that the Lord solves problems for "people who do what is right." And usually, doing what's right means doing the uncomfortable work of confronting our problems sooner rather than later. So with no further ado, Mom, let the problem solving begin . . . today.

What a comfort to know that God is present there
in your life, available to meet every situation with you,
that you are never left to face any problem alone.
Vonette Bright

Never "Just" a Mom

Mighty waters cannot extinguish love;
rivers cannot sweep it away.
Song of Songs 8:7 HCSB

One stay-at-home mother described herself this way: "I'm just a mom." That's like saying, "I'm just an astronaut," or "I'm just a supreme court justice." Motherhood is not just another job. It's one of the most important jobs there is!

As a mother you understand the importance of raising your children with love, with discipline, and with God. You know that your overriding purpose is to care for your children. You know that as you raise those little ones, you're shaping the future. And if you're thinking clearly and following God closely, you know that the Creator will bless your handiwork.

If you're a full-time, stay-at-home mom, you should place a high value on your chosen career; you're never "just a mom." You're fulfilling one of the most important duties on earth . . . and don't ever forget it!

I guess what I've really discovered is the humanizing effect
of children in my life, stretching me, humbling me.
Maybe my thighs aren't as thin as they used to be,
maybe my getaways aren't as glamorous. Still I like
the woman that motherhood has helped me to become.
Susan Lapinski

If You Work Outside the Home

Be strong and brave, and do the work.
Don't be afraid or discouraged, because the LORD God,
my God, is with you. He will not fail you or leave you.
1 Chronicles 28:20 NCV

Nobody ever said that being a working mom was easy! It's tough to hold down a job and raise a family at the same time—tough, but not impossible.

If you're a working mom, you know firsthand that motherhood is perhaps the hardest profession of all. But here are a few hints to make it a little easier:

1. Strive for balance: it's up to you to establish priorities that are important for you and your family.

2. Learn to say no: the word no is one of the greatest timesaving tools ever invented! Use it.

3. Get enough sleep: burning the candle at both ends isn't fun or smart.

4. Get organized: every minute you spend organizing your house can save ten minutes later on. And as a working mom, you deserve all the minutes you can get!

My mother was instrumental in making me believe
that you can accomplish anything if you believe in it.
Wilma Rudolph

Asking and Obeying

Ask in my name, according to my will,
and he'll most certainly give it to you.
Your joy will be a river overflowing its banks!
John 16:24 MSG

God gives the gifts; we, as God's children, should accept them—but often we don't. Why? Because we fail to trust our heavenly Father completely and because we are, at times, surprisingly stubborn.

Stubbornness is a human trait that infects even the most well-meaning among us, almost from birth. We want to do things our own way and in our own time, even if it means disregarding the wisdom of others—including God.

Have you been guilty of doing things your way instead of God's way? If so, you're missing out on some of the Creator's richest blessings. So here's a tip: whenever you have an important choice to make, consult your Father in heaven—heed His advice. Then get ready for God to shower you with more blessings than you can count, because that's precisely what He has promised to do.

There is nothing wrong with asking God's direction.
But it is wrong to go our own way,
then expect Him to bail us out.
Larry Burkett

Multiplying Your Blessings

*The LORD bless you and keep you; the LORD make His
face shine upon you, and be gracious to you.*
Numbers 6:24–25 NKJV

Because you're a mother, you've been specially
blessed by your Father in heaven. God has given
you gifts that are truly too numerous to count. Your
blessings include life, family, freedom, friends, talents,
and possessions, for starters. And now, in response to
those gifts, what will you do? Will you demonstrate
your thanks by thanking God and working hard to
multiply what you've been given? If so, remember
that the gifts you receive from God do just that—they
multiply when you share them with others.

Give thanks to God today for your blessings, and
demonstrate your gratitude by sharing those blessings
with your family, with your friends, and with the
world. When you're willing to put your blessings to
work, there's no limit on how far you can go . . . and
no limit on the fun you'll have getting there.

*Do we not continually pass by blessings innumerable
without notice, and instead fix our eyes on what we feel
to be our trials and our losses, and think and talk about
these until our whole horizon is filled with them,
and we almost begin to think we have no blessings at all?*
Hannah Whitall Smith

A Mother's Work

Fix these words of mine in your hearts and minds. . . .
Teach them to your children, talking about them when you
sit at home and when you walk along the road,
when you lie down and when you get up.
Deuteronomy 11:18–19 NIV

OK, Mom, when does your workday end? Do you wrap things up when the sun goes down, or is sunset simply a regularly scheduled reminder that you'd better step up the pace? If you're like most moms, your duties begin with the alarm clock's ring and end with lights out. And truth be told, you probably wouldn't have it any other way. You find joy in being a mom.

As the amazing mother of your amazing kids, you know that while the duties of motherhood are great, the rewards are even greater. So today, as you pause to thank God for His many blessings, thank Him, too, for the privilege of being a mother. No job on earth is more important . . . or, for that matter, more rewarding.

The woman who creates
and sustains a home is a creator second only to God.
Helen Hunt Jackson

September

A Thank-You Hug for Mom

Dear Mom,

Thanks for listening to our dreams—and thanks for believing in them. When we summoned the courage to confide in you, you supported us, you encouraged us, and you trusted us. If you harbored any doubts, you hid them.

Please know that your faith was effective—because you believed in us, we can have faith and believe in our dreams too.

Living Courageously

We can say with confidence, "The Lord is my helper,
so I will not be afraid. What can mere mortals do to me?"
Hebrews 13:6 NLT

Life can be difficult and discouraging at times. Yet during our darkest moments, we can depend on God. When we do, we find the courage to face even the darkest days with hopeful hearts and willing hands.

Are you ready to do as God asks and lay all your pain, desires, fears, and hopes at His feet? If you can do that, you'll discover a newfound strength, compliments of your heavenly Father.

So when you find yourself worried about the challenges of today or the uncertainties of tomorrow, ask yourself whether you're ready to place your concerns and your life in God's all-powerful, all-knowing, all-loving hands. If the answer to that question is yes—as it should be—then you can draw courage today from the Source of strength that never fails.

With each new experience of letting God be in control,
we gain courage and reinforcement
for daring to do it again and again.
Gloria Gaither

If You Become Discouraged

*Do not be afraid or discouraged, for the LORD
is the one who goes before you. He will be with you;
he will neither fail you nor forsake you.*
Deuteronomy 31:8 NLT

E ven the most upbeat moms can become discouraged
. . . even you. After all, you live in a world where
expectations are sometimes unrealistically high. And
if, for any reason, you fall short, you can start feeling blue in a hurry. That's understandable, yet you're
smart enough to know that blue feelings are unlikely
to solve anything.

The next time you face a big-time disappointment,
face it head on. Don't give in, or up. Instead, assess
your situation realistically and try to improve it. And
while you're at it, have a sincere chat with God,
because He probably has a suggestion or two.

God wants you to stop focusing on your fears and
to trust Him. He is a God of possibility, not negativity.
You can be sure that He will guide you through your
difficulties—and beyond them.

*If I am asked how we are to get rid of discouragements,
I can only say, as I have had to say of so many
other wrong spiritual habits, we must give them up.*
Hannah Whitall Smith

Strength for Today

Those who hope in the LORD will renew their strength.
They will soar on wings like eagles; they will run
and not grow weary, they will walk and not be faint.
Isaiah 40:31 NIV

Where do you go to find strength? The gym? health-food store? espresso bar? chocolate shop? These places are all fine, but there's a better source of strength, and that source is God. He can be a never-ending source of power and courage if you call upon Him.

Are you a spiritually energized mom? Have you tapped in to the power of God? Have you turned your life and your heart over to Him, or are you still muddling along under your own power? If the latter is true, you're missing out on much of the strength you need for today. So start tapping in—and remember that when it comes to strength, God is the ultimate Source.

Worry does not empty tomorrow of its sorrow;
it empties today of its strength.
Corrie ten Boom

September 4

Faith and Family

The fundamental fact of existence is that this trust
in God, this faith, is the firm foundation
under everything that makes life worth living.
Hebrews 11:1 MSG

Would you like to strengthen the ties that bind your family together? Here's a wonderful place to start: strengthen your faith in God.

Every life and every family is a series of successes and failures, celebrations and disappointments, joys and sorrows. Every step of the way, through every triumph and tragedy, God will stand by your family and strengthen each member . . . if you let Him.

When you and your loved ones place your faith, your trust, indeed your lives in the hands of the Creator, you'll be amazed at the marvelous things He can do through you. So strengthen your faith and your family through worship, through Bible study, and through prayer. And trust God's plans. With Him all things are possible, and He stands ready to open a world of possibilities to you and yours . . . if you have faith.

For whatever life holds for you and your family
in the coming days, weave the unfailing fabric of
God's Word through your heart and mind.
It will hold strong, even if the rest of life unravels.
Gigi Graham Tchividjian

Making the Grade

The good person is generous and lends lavishly.
Psalm 112:5 MSG

If your family were being graded on generosity, how would you score? Would you earn As in philanthropy and humility? Hopefully so. But if your grades could stand a little improvement, today is the perfect day to begin.

In this uncertain world, you may feel the urge to hoard your blessings. But don't do it. Instead, give generously to your neighbors, and do so without fanfare. Find someone who has a need, and humbly fill it. Lend a helping hand and share a word of kindness without expecting rewards or accolades. This is God's way.

Pledge today to be a cheerful, generous, courageous giver, and encourage your children to do likewise. The world needs your family's help, and you'll benefit from the spiritual rewards that will be yours when, with a cheerful heart, you share your possessions, your talents, and your time.

I have held many things in my hands,
and I have lost them all; but whatever I have placed
in God's hands, that I still possess.
Martin Luther

The Blessings of Obedience

Good people will have rich blessings.
Proverbs 10:6 NCV

God has given us a guidebook for righteous living; it's called the Bible, and it contains thorough instructions that, if followed, bring us a wide array of rewards and blessings.

The Bible instructs us that a righteous life has many components: faith, honesty, generosity, love, kindness, humility, gratitude, and worship, to name but a few. And if we seek to please the Creator, we must, to the best of our abilities, live according to the principles contained in His Word.

As a loving mother, you're keenly aware that God has entrusted you with a profound responsibility: caring for the needs of your family—including their spiritual needs. To better fulfill that responsibility, study God's Word and live by it. When you do, your example will be a blessing not only to your loved ones but also to generations yet unborn.

We refuse to believe His promises of happiness
and fruitfulness as rewards for obedience.
And we covet His preeminent holiness for ourselves,
wanting to make our own decisions and enthroning
ourselves as equal to God Himself.
Dorothy Kelley Patterson

Actions and Beliefs

*If the way you live isn't consistent with what you believe,
then it's wrong.*
Romans 14:23 MSG

In describing one's beliefs, actions are far better descriptors than words. Yet far too many of us spend more energy talking about our beliefs than living by them—with predictable consequences.

Is your life a picture book of your creed? Are your actions congruent with your beliefs? Are you willing to practice the philosophy you preach?

Today and every day, make certain your actions are guided by God's Word and by the conscience He has placed in your heart. Don't treat your faith as if it were separate from your everyday life. Weave your beliefs into the fabric of your day. When you do these things, Mom, God will honor your good works, and your good works will honor God.

*I say if it's going to be done, let's do it.
Let's not put it in the hands of fate.
Let's take a deep breath and go ahead.*
Anita Baker

Guarding Your Heart

Guard your heart above all else, for it is the source of life.
Proverbs 4:23 HCSB

You are near and dear to God. He loves you more than you can imagine, and He wants the best for you. And one more thing: God wants you to guard your heart—but the world may tempt you to let down your guard.

The world has a way of capturing your attention and distorting your thoughts. Society wants you and your loved ones to focus on worldly matters. God, on the other hand, wants you to focus on Him.

Your task is to make sure you focus your thoughts and energies on God and His priorities, things that enrich your life and enhance your faith. So today, Mom, be watchful and obedient. Guard your heart by giving it to your heavenly Father; it's safe with Him.

The location of your affections will drive
the direction of your decisions.
Lisa Bevere

Asking God

When a believing person prays, great things happen.
James 5:16 NCV

James 5:16 contains a promise: when you pray earnestly, fervently, and often, great things will happen. And it's a promise God will keep. Too many people, however, are too timid or too pessimistic to ask God to do big things. Don't count yourself among their number.

God can and will do great things through you if you have the courage to ask Him . . . and the determination to keep asking Him. So do yourself and your family a big favor by asking God for big things. Then expect Him to do big things. Trust that He can work miracles in your own life and in the lives of your loved ones. But don't expect Him to do all the work. When you do your part, He'll do His part. And when the two of you are working together, you have every right to expect a miracle.

You pay God a compliment by asking great things of Him.
Saint Teresa of Ávila

Another Day,
Another Bunch of Opportunities

As we have opportunity, we must work for the good of all,
especially for those who belong to the household of faith.
Galatians 6:10 HCSB

Mom, are you living the triumphant life God has promised to those who follow Him? Or are you something of a spiritual shrinking violet? As you ponder that question, consider this: God doesn't intend for you to live a life that is merely mediocre. And He doesn't want you to "hide your light." He wants you to "Let your light so shine before men, that they may see your good works and glorify your Father in heaven" (Matthew 5:16 NKJV). In short, God wants you to live a triumphal life so that others might know precisely what it means to follow Him.

Your life should be akin to a victory celebration, a daily exercise in thanksgiving and praise. So join that celebration today . . . and be sure to let everyone around you know that you've joined.

Life is a gift from God,
and we must treasure it, protect it, and invest it.
Warren Wiersbe

Neighbors

Show family affection to one another with brotherly love. Outdo one another in showing honor. Do not lack diligence; be fervent in spirit; serve the Lord. Rejoice in hope; be patient in affliction; be persistent in prayer.

Romans 12:10–12 HCSB

Neighbors: we know that we're supposed to love them, and yet there's so little time . . . and we're so busy. No matter. We are instructed to love our neighbors just as we love ourselves. In God's Word we're not asked to love our neighbors; nor are we encouraged to do so. We are commanded to love them. Period.

This very day, Mom, you will encounter someone who needs a word of encouragement, a pat on the back, a helping hand, or a heartfelt prayer. And if you don't reach out to that person, who will? If you don't take the time to understand the needs of those around you, who will? If you don't love your fellow human beings, who will? So look for a neighbor in need . . . and then do something to help.

If my heart is right with God,
every human being is my neighbor.
Oswald Chambers

Keeping Things in Perspective

*All I'm doing right now, friends, is showing how these
things pertain to Apollos and me so that you will learn
restraint and not rush into making judgments without
knowing all the facts. It's important to look at things from
God's point of view. I would rather not see you inflating or
deflating reputations based on mere hearsay.*

1 Corinthians 4:6 MSG

For most of us life is busy and complicated. Amid
the rush and crush of the daily grind, it's easy to
lose perspective . . . easy, but detrimental. When our
world seems to be spinning out of control, we can
regain perspective by slowing down and turning our
thoughts and prayers toward God.

So here's a question for you, Mom: are you
determined to keep things in perspective, and have
you made up your mind to teach your children to
do likewise? If so, you'll be happy you did—and so
will they.

When you focus on your blessings, not your
misfortunes, God will smile on you and yours. So do
yourself and your loved ones a favor: learn to think
optimistically about the world you live in and the life
you lead. Then prepare for the blessings that are sure
to come.

*The proper perspective creates within us a spirit of
reaching outside of ourselves with joy and enthusiasm.*
Luci Swindoll

Always Ready

*Watch therefore, and pray always
that you may be counted worthy.*
Luke 21:36 NKJV

Jesus made it clear to His disciples that they should pray always. And so should we. Genuine, heartfelt prayer changes things—and it changes us. When we lift our hearts to our Father in heaven, we open ourselves to a never-ending source of divine wisdom and infinite love.

Do you have questions you can't answer? Ask for the guidance of your Creator. Whatever your need, no matter how great or small, pray about it. When you do, you can be certain that God hears you.

God is not distant; He's right here, Mom, watching after you and your loved ones. His hand is guiding and shaping your family, your community, and your world. He's always ready to talk with you. Are you ready to talk to Him?

*We must leave it to God to answer our prayers
in His own wisest way. Sometimes we are so impatient
and think that God does not answer. God always answers!
He never fails! Be still. Abide in Him.*
Mrs. Charles E. Cowman

Living on Purpose

You're sons of Light, daughters of Day.
We live under wide open skies and know where we stand.
So let's not sleepwalk through life.
1 Thessalonians 5:5–6 MSG

Life is best lived on purpose. And purpose, like everything else in the universe, begins with God. Whether you realize it or not, God has a plan for your life, a divine calling, a direction in which He is leading you. When you welcome God into your heart and establish a genuine relationship with Him, He will begin, in time, to make His purposes known.

Sometimes God's intentions will be clear to you; other times His plan will seem mysterious. But even on those days when you're unsure which way to turn, never lose sight of these overarching truths: God created you for a reason; He has important work for you to do; and He's waiting patiently for you to do it.

The next step, Mom, is up to you.

The one predominant duty is to find one's work
and to do it.
Charlotte Perkins Gilman

Encouraging Words
for Family and Friends

*Two are better than one because they have
a good reward for their efforts. For if either falls,
his companion can lift him up; but pity the one who
falls without another to lift him up.*
Ecclesiastes 4:9–10 HCSB

Life is a team sport, and all of us need occasional pats on the back from our teammates. Whether you realize it or not, many of the people you encounter each day are in desperate need of a smile or an encouraging word. The world can be a rough place, and you never know which acquaintances, friends, and family members feel troubled by the challenges of everyday life.

Since it's not always obvious who needs your help, the best strategy is to try to encourage all the people who cross your path. So here's something you can do, Mom—make this promise to yourself and keep it: Vow to be a source of encouragement to everyone you meet. Share your optimism with family members, friends, coworkers, and even with strangers. Never has the need been greater.

*We do have the ability to encourage or discourage each
other with the words we say. In order to maintain a
positive mood, our hearts must be in good condition.*
Annie Chapman

His Healing Touch

"I will give peace, real peace, to those far and near,
and I will heal them," says the LORD.
Isaiah 57:19 NCV

Mom, are you concerned about your spiritual, physical, or emotional health? If so, there's a timeless source of comfort and assurance that's as near as your next breath. That source of insight and comfort is God.

God is concerned about every aspect of your life, including your health. And when you face concerns of any sort—including health-related issues—God is with you.

So trust your medical doctor to do his or her part, and turn to your family and friends for moral, physical, and spiritual support. But before you do anything else, place your trust in your benevolent, heavenly Father for the ultimate source of strength, protection, and wisdom. His healing touch, like His love, endures forever.

God helps the sick in two ways, through the science of
medicine and through the science of faith and prayer.
Norman Vincent Peale

Standing Up for Yourself

Be alert, stand firm in the faith, be brave and strong.
1 Corinthians 16:13 HCSB

Because you're a mother, you can demonstrate to your children the importance of assertiveness. But if you haven't quite learned the fine art of standing up for yourself, you're not alone—plenty of people, even people who have stood up for themselves in the past, could use a brushup on their assertiveness skills.

Assertiveness is an essential component of a strong character. When it's expressed appropriately, assertiveness can help you stand on your own two feet. But without a healthy dose of it, you may be doomed to follow the crowd wherever they choose to go (and often they choose to go in the wrong direction).

You're never too old to learn how to become a more assertive person. So do yourself this major-league favor: learn to say no politely, firmly, and whenever necessary. You'll not only be a better person, but you'll also be a better example to your children.

You must learn to say no when something
is not right for you.
Leontyne Price

Limitless Love

Praise the LORD, all nations! Glorify Him, all peoples!
For great is His faithful love to us;
the LORD's faithfulness endures forever. Hallelujah!
Psalm 117 HCSB

Because God's power is limitless, it's far beyond the comprehension of mortal minds. But even though we can't fully understand the immensity of God, we can be open to His love.

God's ability to love is not fettered with temporal boundaries or earthly limitations. The love that flows from the heart of God is infinite—and today presents yet another opportunity for you to celebrate that love.

As you carve out quiet moments of thanksgiving and praise for your heavenly Father, open yourself to His presence and His love. He is here, waiting. His love is here, always.

You are a glorious creation, a unique individual, a beautiful example of God's handiwork. And God's love for you is limitless, Mom. Accept that love, acknowledge it, and be grateful.

I am convinced our hearts are not healthy until they have
been satisfied by the only completely healthy love
that exists: the love of God Himself.
Beth Moore

With You Always

I am not alone, because the Father is with Me.
John 16:32 HCSB

Where is God? God is eternally with us. He is omnipresent. He is, quite literally, everywhere you've ever been and everywhere you will ever go. He's with you night and day; He knows your every thought; He hears your every heartbeat.

Sometimes, under the crush of your maternal duties, God may seem far away. Or, when the disappointments and sorrows of life leave you brokenhearted, God may seem distant to you. But He's not. When you earnestly seek God, you will find Him, because He is right there by your side, waiting patiently for you to reach out to Him . . . right now.

What God promises is that He always, always comes.
He always shows up. He always saves.
He always rescues. His timing is not ours.
His methods are usually unconventional.
But what we can know, what we can settle in our soul,
is that He is faithful to come when we call.
Angela Thomas

God's Timing

*Wait for the LORD; be courageous
and let your heart be strong. Wait for the LORD.*
Psalm 27:14 HCSB

If you're in a hurry for good things to happen to you and your family, you're not the only mom on the block who feels that way. But sometimes you'll simply have to be patient.

God has created a world that unfolds according to His timetable, not ours . . . thank goodness! We mortals would make a terrible mess of things. But God knows what He's doing.

Of course, God's plans don't always unfold according to our wishes or at the time of our own choosing. Nonetheless, we can trust the benevolent, all-knowing Father as we wait patiently for Him to reveal Himself. Until God's plans are made clear to us, our task is simply to walk in faith and never lose hope, knowing that His ways are always best.

*Waiting on God brings us to the journey's end
quicker than our feet.*
Mrs. Charles E. Cowman

Always Hopeful

We are saved by hope.
Romans 8:24 KJV

As we all know, hope can be a perishable commodity. Despite God's promises, and despite the countless blessings we've received, we are frail and fearful human beings, and we lose hope from time to time. When we do, we need the encouragement of close friends and family members . . . and we need the reassuring touch of God's hand.

Even though this world can be a place of trials and struggles, God has promised us peace, joy, and eternal life if we entrust our lives to Him.

Are you a mother who asks God to move mountains in your life, or are you stumbling over molehills? Ask for help from the Almighty today—with faith and with fervor, not being afraid to hope—and then watch in amazement as your mountains begin to move.

The most profane word we use is hopeless.
When you say a situation or person is hopeless,
you are slamming the door in the face of God.
Kathy Troccoli

Judging Others

Do not judge, or you too will be judged.
For in the same way you judge others, you will be judged,
and with the measure you use, it will be measured to you.
Matthew 7:1 NIV

OK, Mom, answer honestly: are you one of those people who finds it easy to judge others? (Plenty of us do.) If so, it's time to make radical changes in the way you view the world and the people in it.

When considering the shortcomings of others, remember this: in matters of judgment, God doesn't need (or want) your help. Why? Because God is perfectly capable of judging the human heart . . . and you're not.

All of us have fallen short of God's standard of perfection, so none of us is qualified to "cast the first stone." Thankfully, God has forgiven us; and we must forgive others. Let us refrain, then, from judging our family members, our friends, and others around us. Instead, let's forgive them and love them in the same way God has forgiven and loves us.

God is the only judge. You are just His emissary of peace.
Saint Thérèse of Lisieux

Looking for Miracles

I am the Alpha and the Omega, the Beginning
and the End. I will give to the thirsty
from the spring of living water as a gift.
Revelation 21:6 HCSB

If you haven't seen any of God's miracles lately, perhaps you haven't been looking. Throughout history the Creator has intervened in the course of human events in ways that cannot be explained by science or human rationale. And He's still doing so today.

God's miracles are not limited to special occasions, nor are they witnessed only by a select few. God is crafting His wonders all around us: the miracle of a newborn baby; the miracle of a world renewing itself with every sunrise; the miracle of lives transformed by God's love and grace. Each day God's handiwork is evident for all to see and experience.

Today, Mom, seize the opportunity to observe God's hand at work. His miracles come in a variety of shapes and sizes, so keep your eyes and your heart open. Don't become jaded by the world's pessimism; miracles are real, and they're happening all around you. Be watchful and you'll soon be amazed.

God specializes in things thought impossible.
Catherine Marshall

Patience and More Patience

God blesses the people who patiently endure testing.
Afterward they will receive the crown of life that God
has promised to those who love him.
James 1:12 NLT

Family life demands patience—and lots of it. We live in imperfect homes inhabited by imperfect kids and their imperfect parents. Thank goodness family life doesn't have to be perfect to be wonderful!

Sometimes we inherit troubles from other folks (some of whom live under our roofs and some who don't). On other occasions we create trouble for ourselves. In either case, what we need to get through our rough spots is patience.

So here's a reminder, Mom: the next time you find your patience pushed to the limit by the limitations of others, remember that nobody is perfect (including you). And remember that the less you focus on people's imperfections, the better things will be both for them and for you.

Expect trouble as an inevitable part of life
and repeat to yourself the most comforting words of all:
this, too, shall pass.
Ann Landers

Work and Good Luck

Thanks be to God for His indescribable gift!
2 Corinthians 9:15 NKJV

It's an old idea, and a true one: the harder you work, the "luckier" you are. As a mother you certainly know a few things about both sides of that equation—you know quite a lot about work and just as much about what some call luck.

The fact that you're on the job fulfilling your role as a responsible mom means you're working from dawn to dusk. It also means you're incredibly fortunate to be the mother of your kids.

Your family is a unique blessing from the Creator, a gift He expects you to cherish and care for. So say a prayer of thanks today for the job of being a mom. And as you think about your personal mixture of hard work and good fortune, thank God for both.

Motherhood is the biggest on-the-job training
program in existence today.
Erma Bombeck

Exciting Possibilities

All things are possible for the one who believes.
Mark 9:23 NCV

Are you genuinely excited about life and about the opportunities God has placed before you? Do you know your Creator as a God of infinite possibilities, and are you energized by that realization? If so, you're a wise woman. But if you've been living under a cloud of doubt, or if you're unsure why you should be excited about this day (and all the ones that follow it), God probably would like to have a little chat with you.

God's Word teaches us that all things are possible through Him. Do you believe that, Mom? If you do, then you can face the future with a delicious blend of excitement and delight.

God's power isn't limited; and because of that, neither are the possibilities He can open up in your life—and the sooner you realize it, the sooner you can take advantage of His gifts and start building a better life for you and your loved ones.

A possibility is a hint from God.
Søren Kierkegaard

Taking Your Troubles to God

Anyone who is having troubles should pray.
James 5:13 NCV

Every family encounters tough times, and your family is no exception. When Old Man Trouble arrives on your doorstep, it's probably time to take your troubles to God—in prayer—and leave them there.

Mom, is the habit of prayer an integral part of your daily life, or is it something of a hit and miss? Do you "pray without ceasing," or do you talk to God less frequently than that?

Daily prayer and meditation is a matter of will and habit. We must willingly organize our time by carving out quiet moments with God, and we must form the habit of daily worship. When we do, we'll discover that on good days and on not-so-good days, God is always ready to hear and to help.

We must pray literally without ceasing, in every occurrence and employment of our lives. You know I mean that prayer of the heart which is independent of place or situation, or which is, rather, a habit of lifting up the heart to God, as in a constant communication with Him.

Saint Elizabeth Ann Seton

Noble Plans

A noble person plans noble things;
he stands up for noble causes.
Isaiah 32:8 HCSB

Mom, here's a two-part question: will you summon the courage to make noble plans for the future, and will you encourage your loved ones to do likewise? Hopefully, you'll answer with a resounding yes, and yes.

God has a noble plan for your life, an important plan, a plan that only you can fulfill. But there's a catch: you live in a world that entices you to squander your resources and your time in a real-life version of Trivial Pursuit. The temptation to pursue trivialities is one you should avoid.

Instead of focusing on things that won't matter much in the long run, make worthy plans, set worthy goals, and get busy turning those goals into reality. Don't settle for second best, and don't sell yourself short. Even if your goals seem to stretch you to the limit, don't be discouraged. No goal is too big and no plan is too ambitious for you and God—working together—to accomplish.

A good goal is like a strenuous exercise—
it makes you stretch.
Mary Kay Ash

The Best Time to Apologize

He who loves a quarrel loves sin.
Proverbs 17:19 NIV

Do you owe anyone an apology? If not, you're to be congratulated for being a thoughtful friend and a marvelous mom. But if you're like most of us, you may have a few people to whom you owe a heartfelt "I'm sorry." If so, the best time to apologize is now.

For some strange reason, many of us have a tough time saying we're sorry. We feel as if we're being forced to swallow our pride, and we stubbornly refuse to do it. But the more we put off the inevitable, the more emotional baggage we carry around . . . and attach to the apologies we should have offered a long time ago.

Today make a list of any folks who are owed an apology by you. And then do the right thing. They'll probably be happy you did, but you'll be even happier. So why deprive yourself of that reward a moment longer?

Confession of our faults is the next best thing to innocence.
Publilius Syrus

The Language Our Kids Should Hear

Watch the way you talk. Let nothing foul or dirty come out of your mouth. Say only what helps, each word a gift.
Ephesians 4:29 MSG

The popularity of profanity seems at an all-time high, and the trend line is rising. Everywhere we turn, we're confronted with words (and images) that are inappropriate even for grownups, not to mention kids.

So what's a mother to do? Well, you can't raise your kid in a convent, but here are a few simple things you can do: (1) Make sure your child never hears you say something you wouldn't want him or her to repeat. (2) Make sure adults and children alike understand that your home is a profanity-free zone. (3) Don't allow inappropriate television shows, commercials, or movies to be displayed on your TV (or computer) screens.

When you do these things, you'll help make your house an island of civility in a sea of bad taste. You can't change the world, but you can exercise control over what's seen and said in your home.

The battle of the tongue is won not in the mouth but in the heart.
Annie Chapman

October

A Thank-You Hug for Mom

Dear Mom,

Thanks for your patience. The rigors of motherhood can test the patience of the most even-tempered moms, but you passed with flying colors.

All of us, parents and children alike, make our share of mistakes. When we made our mistakes, you dried our tears, you forgave us, and you convinced us that we could recover. We thank God for your patience, for your faith, and for your love.

Taking Out the Mental Garbage

*Fix your thoughts on what is true and honorable
and right. Think about things that are pure and lovely
and admirable. Think about things that are
excellent and worthy of praise.*
Philippians 4:8 NLT

Mental garbage has a way of gradually building up in the minds of even the most optimistic moms, so let this serve as a reminder to keep yourself on guard against that messy collection of negative thoughts, wrongheaded ideas, irrational notions, and unhelpful ruminations that can swirl around in your brain. Those kinds of thoughts can turn your mind into the psychological equivalent of a landfill.

When you feel that your healthy meditations have morphed into sloppy thinking, it's time to take out the garbage by talking to someone you can trust . . . starting with God. He'll help you recycle those bad thoughts and turn them into good ones.

So the next time your thoughts migrate toward the negative end of the spectrum, do the healthy thing: open up your mind . . . and take out the trash.

*If you have a negative thought, don't waste hours
thinking about it. Simply direct yourself
to something positive and keep repeating the positive
until you eliminate the negative.*
Tina Louise

Never Too Heavy

These things I have spoken to you, that in Me you may have peace. In the world you will have tribulation; but be of good cheer, I have overcome the world.
John 16:33 NKJV

As we travel the roads of life, all of us meet what seem to be dead ends. When we do, we may become discouraged. After all, we live in a society that wants to live on easy street.

If you're experiencing difficult circumstances or profound disappointments, remember that God is watching over you, and He will never ask you to carry a load that's too heavy for you.

So the next time you're asked to shoulder a heavy burden, remember there's a good way and a bad way to carry every load. The best way is to keep working, keep believing, and never give in to discouragement. With God no load is too heavy.

Success actually becomes a habit through the determined overcoming of obstacles as we meet them one by one.
Laura Ingalls Wilder

Learning from Experiences

*Prefer my life-disciplines over chasing after money,
and God-knowledge over a lucrative career.
For Wisdom is better than all the trappings of wealth;
nothing you could wish for holds a candle to her.*
Proverbs 8:10–11 MSG

Mom, have you ever found yourself enrolled in the school of hard knocks? If so, you probably learned a lesson or two that you swore you'd never forget. But the question of the day is this: have you really learned from your experiences, or have you (like most of us) found yourself, on occasion, making the same old mistakes?

All experiences, both good and bad, can teach us. But it's up to each of us to make sure we're observant enough—and sensible enough—to be taught. So take time today to consider the lessons God may still be trying to teach you. Think about the lessons you've learned and the ones that need to be relearned. And remember this: when it comes to learning from your experiences, sooner is better than later . . . and permanent is better than temporary.

*We live in the present, we dream of the future,
but we learn eternal truths from the past.*
Lucy Maud Montgomery

Too Busy

Don't burn out; keep yourselves fueled and aflame.
Be alert servants of the Master, cheerfully expectant.
Don't quit in hard times; pray all the harder.
Romans 12:11–12 MSG

It's been said before, but it's worth saying again: the things that matter most must never be at the mercy of the things that matter least. So how will you choose to organize the busy day ahead? Will you rush from place to place with scarcely a moment to spare, or will you slow down enough to make time for the things that really matter?

The world wants you to believe there's enough time to "have it all"—that there's plenty of time to meet every obligation and finish every task. But it's not true; you really don't have time for everything. It's up to you, Mom, to invest your life in the important things.

Today, before you rush headlong into the fray, take a few moments to think about your priorities . . . and schedule your time accordingly.

Getting things accomplished isn't nearly
as important as taking time for love.
Janette Oke

Choices

I am offering you life or death, blessings or curses.
Now, choose life! . . . To choose life is to love the LORD
your God, obey him, and stay close to him.
Deuteronomy 30:19–20 NCV

Every life, including yours, is a tapestry of choices made. So the beauty and quality of that tapestry depends, to a large extent, on the quality of the choices you make.

Would you like to enjoy a life of abundance and significance? If so, make choices that are pleasing to God.

From the instant you wake up in the morning until the moment you nod off to sleep at night, you make lots of decisions: decisions about the things you do, decisions about the words you speak, and decisions about the thoughts you entertain.

Today, Mom, it's up to you (and only you) to make wise choices . . . choices that enhance your relationship with God and, as a result, your quality of life.

Your heart often knows things before your mind does.
Polly Adler

Showing Courtesy

Be hospitable to one another without grumbling.
1 Peter 4:9 NKJV

Here in the twenty-first century, it sometimes seems like common courtesy is a decidedly uncommon trait. But if we are to trust the Bible—and we should—then we'll understand that kindness and courtesy will never go out of style. Your challenge, as a thoughtful mother, is to make sure it never goes out of style at your house.

Today be a little kinder than necessary, and encourage your kids to behave in like manner. Make sure you and yours offer the gift of courtesy to family members, to friends, and even to people you don't know personally. Be gentle, considerate, and well-mannered. And as you remember all the gracious things God has done for you, offer the return courtesy of honoring Him with your words and with your deeds. He expects no less; He deserves no less; and He wants no less for the folks who cross your path.

Reach out and care for someone who needs the touch of hospitality. The time you spend caring today will be a love gift that will blossom into the fresh joy of God's Spirit in the future.
Emilie Barnes

Teaching the Rewards of Discipline

Apply your heart to discipline,
and your ears to words of knowledge.
Proverbs 23:12 NASB

Wise moms (like you) teach their children the importance of discipline, using both words and examples, with a decided emphasis on example. After all, life's greatest rewards seldom fall into our laps; our greatest accomplishments usually require lots of work. But with God's help, we're up to the task.

God has big plans for us, plans that He knows we can accomplish if we're willing to work hard and work smart.

The world often conspires to teach our kids that it's OK to look for shortcuts. But as concerned parents we must teach our children that success is earned by working hard, not by "getting by." Our youngsters must never expect their rewards to precede their labors. But when we teach our kids to work diligently and consistently, they can expect to earn rich rewards for their efforts.

Some people regard discipline as a chore.
For me, it is a kind of order that sets me free to fly.
Julie Andrews

Beyond Envy

*Let us not become boastful, challenging one another,
envying one another.*
Galatians 5:26 NASB

In a competitive, cut-throat world, it's easy to become envious of others' success. But it's wrong.

We know intuitively that envy is wrong, but because we're frail, imperfect human beings, we sometimes struggle with feelings of envy. These feelings may be especially forceful when we see other people experience unusually good fortune.

Have you recently felt the pangs of envy creeping into your heart? If so, it's time to focus on the marvelous things God has done for you and your family. And just as importantly, refrain from preoccupying yourself with the blessings God has chosen to give others.

Want a surefire formula for a happier, healthier life? Count your own blessings and let your neighbors count theirs. It's the peaceful way to live.

Discontent dries up the soul.
Elisabeth Elliot

God First

Honor G\OD with everything you own;
give him the first and the best. Your barns will burst,
your wine vats will brim over.
Proverbs 3:9–10 MSG

As you think about the nature of your relationship with God, remember this: you will always have some type of relationship with Him. It's inevitable that your life will be lived in relationship to God. The question is not if you will have a relationship with Him; the burning question is whether that relationship will be one that seeks to honor Him.

Are you willing to place God first in your life? Unless you can honestly answer this question with a resounding Yes! then your relationship with God isn't what it could be, or what it should be. Thankfully, God is always available; He's always ready to forgive, and He's waiting to hear from you now. The rest, Mom, is up to you.

To yield to God means to belong to God,
and to belong to God means to have all
His infinite power. To belong to God means to have all.
Hannah Whitall Smith

A Spiritual Sickness

*If you harbor bitter envy and selfish ambition
in your hearts, do not boast about it or deny the truth.
Such "wisdom" does not come down from heaven
but is earthly, unspiritual.*

James 3:14–15 NIV

Bitterness is a spiritual sickness. It will consume your soul; it is dangerous to your emotional health. It can destroy you if you let it . . . so don't let it!

If you're caught up in anger or resentment, you know all too well the destructive power of these emotions. How can you rid yourself of these feelings? First, prayerfully ask God to cleanse your heart. Then learn to catch yourself and redirect your thinking and attitude whenever thoughts of bitterness or hatred attack you. Your challenge is this: learn to resist negative thoughts before they hijack your emotions.

When you learn to focus your thoughts on more positive (and rational) topics, you'll be protected from the spiritual and emotional consequences of bitterness . . . and you'll be wiser, healthier, and happier too. So, Mom, why wait? Defeat destructive bitterness today.

*Life appears to me too short to be spent in nursing
animosity or registering wrong.*

Charlotte Brontë

The Rewards of Integrity

The integrity of the upright guides them,
but the unfaithful are destroyed by their duplicity.
Proverbs 11:3 NIV

The Bible makes it clear that God rewards integrity, but duplicity brings destruction. So if we seek to earn the kind of lasting rewards God bestows on those who obey Him, we must make honesty the hallmark of our dealings with others.

Character is built slowly over a lifetime. It's the sum of every right decision, every honest word, every noble thought, and every heartfelt prayer. It's built upon a foundation of industry, generosity, and humility. Character is a precious thing—difficult to build but easy to tear down. As a caring mother, you'll want to live each day with discipline, honesty, and faith. When you do, integrity becomes a habit. And God smiles.

Maintaining your integrity in a world of sham
is no small accomplishment.
Wayne Oates

What's Really Important

Anyone trusting in his riches will fall,
but the righteous will flourish like foliage.
Proverbs 11:28 HCSB

In the demanding world in which we live, financial prosperity can be a good thing, but spiritual prosperity is profoundly more important. Yet our society leads us to believe otherwise. The world glorifies material possessions, personal fame, and physical beauty above all else. These things, of course, are relatively unimportant to God. God sees the human heart, and that's what matters to Him.

As you establish your priorities for the coming day, remember these truths, Mom: The world will do everything it can to convince you that "things" are important. The world will tempt you to value fortune above faith and possessions above peace. God, on the other hand, wants you to know that your relationship with Him is what's all-important. Trust God.

We are made spiritually lethargic
by a steady diet of materialism.
Mary Morrison Suggs

Complaints

> *Do everything without complaining or arguing.*
> *Then you will be innocent and without any wrong.*
> *Philippians 2:14–15 NCV*

Sometimes we lose sight of our blessings. It's all too easy, unfortunately. Ironically, most of us have more blessings than we can count; but we still find reasons to complain about the little frustrations of everyday life. To do so, of course, is not only unhelpful, it's a serious roadblock on the path to spiritual growth and abundance.

Our complaints seldom accomplish the positive results we hope for. And to make matters worse, when we complain, we surrender our inner strength and burden those around us.

Are you tempted to complain about the inevitable frustrations of everyday living? Don't do it, Mom! Today and every day, make it a practice to count your blessings, not your hardships. It's truly the happiest way to live.

> *Gratitude is riches. Complaint is poverty.*
> *Doris Day*

The Joyful Mom

Light shines on those who do right;
joy belongs to those who are honest. Rejoice in the LORD,
you who do right. Praise his holy name.
Psalm 97:11–12 NCV

Are you a mother whose joy is evident for all to see? Do you spread the seeds of good cheer and celebration wherever you go? If so, congratulations: your joyful spirit serves as a powerful example to your family and friends. And because of your attitude, your children will have good reason to heed the words of Proverbs 31 and "rise up" to call you blessed.

God's plan for you and your clan includes heaping helpings of abundance and joy. Claim these gifts today. And as you do so, remind yourself and your loved ones that God continuously offers more blessings than one family can count. He offers His abundance; He offers His peace; and He offers His joy. All you must do is accept these gifts . . . and share them freely, starting today.

Joy is a by-product not of happy circumstances, education,
or talent, but of a healthy relationship with God
and a determination to love Him no matter what.
Barbara Johnson

When People Are Difficult

Stay away from a foolish man;
you will gain no knowledge from his speech.
Proverbs 14:7 HCSB

Sometimes people can be discourteous and cruel.
Sometimes people can be unfair, unkind, and
unappreciative. Sometimes people get angry and
frustrated. So what's a woman to do when she's
confronted with difficult people? God's answer is
straightforward: forgive, forget, and move on. In
Luke 6:37 Jesus said, "Do not judge, and you will
not be judged. Do not condemn, and you will not
be condemned. Forgive, and you will be forgiven"
(HCSB).

Today and every day, Mom, do your best to be
quick to forgive others for their shortcomings. And
when other people misbehave (as they will from time
to time), don't pay too much attention. Just forgive
those people as quickly as you can and try to move on
. . . as quickly as you can.

Not everybody is healthy enough to have
a front-row seat in your life.
Susan L. Taylor

From Anxiety to Peace

Cast all your anxiety on him because he cares for you.
1 Peter 5:7 NIV

When negative emotions like fear and anxiety separate us from the spiritual blessings God wants to bestow on us, it's time to rethink our priorities and renew our faith. And we must place faith above feelings.

Human emotions are always changing, and they're often unreliable. Our emotions are like the weather, only more fickle. So we must learn to live by faith, not by the ups and downs of our own emotional roller coasters.

Sometime during this day you may be gripped by a strong negative emotion. Maybe you'll be anxious about tomorrow or fearful about the more distant future. But don't let those feelings rule you. Rein them in. Test them. And turn them over to God. Your emotions will vary; God will not. So trust Him completely, and let your anxious feelings fade away as you begin to feel His peace.

*Every tomorrow has two handles: we can take hold
of the handle of anxiety or the handle of faith.*
Henry Ward Beecher

The Trap of Pessimism

Why are you cast down, O my soul? And why are you disquieted within me? Hope in God; for I shall yet praise Him, the help of my countenance and my God.

Psalm 42:11 NKJV

Sometimes, despite our faith in God, we fall into the spiritual traps of worry, discouragement, or weariness, and our hearts become heavy. And at those times what we need is plenty of rest, a good dose of perspective, and God's healing touch.

Pessimism is a trap, Mom—don't fall into it. Instead, make this promise to yourself and keep it: vow to be a hope-filled woman. Think optimistically about your life, your family, your friends, your faith, and your future. Hope in God rather than trusting your fears. Take time to celebrate His glorious creation. And then, when you've filled your heart with hope and gladness, share your renewed optimism with others. Your loved ones will be better for it, and so will you.

The pessimist sees the difficulty in every opportunity; the optimist sees the opportunity in every difficulty.

Lawrence Pearsall Jacks

Forgiveness and Spiritual Growth

Don't insist on getting even; that's not for you to do.
"I'll do the judging," says God. "I'll take care of it."
Romans 12:19 MSG

Forgiveness is an exercise in spiritual growth: the more we forgive, the more we grow. Conversely, bitterness makes spiritual growth impossible: when our hearts are filled with resentment and anger, there's no room left for love.

When we cease to grow, either emotionally or spiritually, we do ourselves and our loved ones a profound disservice. But if we continue to study God's Word, pray, and do our best to live in the center of His will, we won't be stagnant. We'll continue to grow as God intends.

In the quiet moments when we open our hearts to God, the Creator who made us keeps remaking us. He gives us direction, perspective, and wisdom—and He gives us the courage to forgive other folks. After all, judging is God's job, not ours.

Our relationships with other people are of primary
importance to God. Because God is love,
He cannot tolerate any unforgiveness or hardness
in us toward any individual.
Catherine Marshall

Teaching Them to Manage Time

If you are too lazy to plow in the right season,
you will have no food at the harvest.
Proverbs 20:4 NLT

Mom, are you serious about teaching your kids the wisdom of getting things done in a timely manner? And are you willing to teach the "gospel" of getting things done by your example as well as your words? If so, your children will be better for it.

Procrastination is, at its core, a struggle against oneself; and the only antidote is action. Once we acquire the habit of doing what needs to be done when it needs to be done, we avoid untold trouble, worry, and stress. But how do we defeat procrastination? By paying less attention to our fears and more attention to our responsibilities.

Life punishes procrastinators, and it does so sooner rather than later. In other words, Mom, life doesn't procrastinate. And neither should you.

Lost time is like a run in a stocking. It always gets worse.
Anne Morrow Lindbergh

Time for a Hug

For the happy heart, life is a continual feast.
Proverbs 15:15 NLT

Mom, do you know someone who needs a hug (or a smile or a kind word)? Maybe this person is related to you, and maybe not. In either case, it's up to you to do something today—not tomorrow, not next week, but right now.

Of course your calendar is full. You have many obligations, a full to-do list, and many people to care for. No matter. God wants you to share today (not at some point in the distant future) the feast of love and joy He's placed in your heart.

When it comes to planting God's seeds in the soil of eternity, the only certain time we have is now. And when it comes to sharing hugs with our family and friends, there's simply no time like the present.

A hug is the ideal gift . . . one size fits all.
Source Unknown

Attention Please

Whoever becomes simple and elemental again,
like this child, will rank high in God's kingdom.
Matthew 18:4 MSG

Is yours a life of moderation or accumulation? Are you more interested in the possessions you can acquire or in the person you can become? The way you answer these questions today will affect the direction of your life tomorrow and in the more distant future.

Ours is a highly complex society, a place where people and corporations vie for your attention, your time, and your dollars. Don't let them succeed in complicating your life! Keep your eyes focused on God.

If your material possessions are somehow distancing you from God, get back to basics. If your outside interests leave you too little time for your family or your Creator, slow down the merry-go-round or, better yet, step off for a breather. Enjoy the simpler things in life . . . like the company of your heavenly Father. Remember, God wants your full attention, and He wants it today; so don't let anybody or anything get in His way.

I have the greatest of all riches: that of not desiring them.
Eleonora Duse

Giving Thanks to the Creator

In everything give thanks;
for this is the will of God in Christ Jesus for you.
1 Thessalonians 5:18 NKJV

As a busy mom who takes her responsibilities seriously, occasionally you'll find yourself caught up in the demands of everyday living. When that happens, it's understandable that you might, at times, forget to pause and thank your Creator for His blessings. But if the demands of motherhood have caused you to make a habit of ignoring God's gifts, perhaps it's time to reevaluate your routine, your obligations, and your priorities.

Whenever you slow down and express your sincere gratitude to the Father, you enrich your own life and the lives of your loved ones. So thanksgiving should become a habit, a regular part of your day. God has blessed you beyond measure, and for that He deserves your sincere gratitude. So give Him thanks every day . . . starting today.

Life does not have to be perfect to be wonderful.
Annette Funicello

Resisting the Impulse

Ignorant zeal is worthless; haste makes waste.
Proverbs 19:2 MSG

Are you, at times, just a little bit impulsive? Do you occasionally leap before you look? Do you react first and think about your reaction second? If so, God's Word has some advice for you.

In the Bible it's clear that we are to lead lives of discipline, diligence, moderation, and maturity. But the world often tempts us to behave otherwise. Everywhere we turn, it seems, we face powerful temptations to indulge in undisciplined, unruly behaviors—impulse.

God's Word instructs us to be disciplined in our thoughts and our actions; it warns us against the dangers of impulsiveness. Our impulses may lead us astray, but our heavenly Father will not. So if we're wise, we'll learn to slow ourselves down; we'll look (and think) before we leap; and we'll consult God before we make big decisions, not after.

> *We will always experience regret when we live*
> *for the moment and do not weigh our words*
> *and deeds before we give them life.*
> Lisa Bevere

The World and You

*Don't copy the behavior and customs of this world,
but let God transform you into a new person
by changing the way you think.*
Romans 12:2 NLT

We live in the world, but we must not worship it. Our duty is to place God first and everything else second. But because we are imperfect human beings with imperfect faith, keeping God in His rightful place is often difficult. In fact, at every turn, we're tempted to let Him fall somewhere further down our list of priorities.

The twenty-first-century world is a noisy, distracting place filled with countless opportunities for us and our family members to stray from God. The cry seems to come from everywhere: "Worship me with your time, your money, your energy, and your thoughts!" But only God is deserving of all those things. And He instructs us to worship Him first and to love our neighbors as we love ourselves; everything else must be secondary.

*Every day, I find countless opportunities to decide
whether I will obey God and demonstrate my love
for Him or try to please myself or the world system.
God is waiting for my choices.*
Bill Bright

Real Prosperity

*Serving God does make us very rich, if we are satisfied
with what we have. We brought nothing into the world,
so we can take nothing out. But, if we have food
and clothes, we will be satisfied with that.*
1 Timothy 6:6–8 NCV

We live in an era of prosperity, a time when many of us have been richly blessed with an assortment of material possessions that our forebears scarcely could have imagined. As moms living in this abundant age, we must be cautious; we must keep prosperity in perspective.

The world stresses the importance of material possessions, but God doesn't. The world promises happiness through wealth and acclaim; God promises peace through His Son.

The world often makes promises it cannot keep, but when God makes a promise, He keeps it—not just for a day or a year or a lifetime, but for all eternity. So today, Mom, choose God's kind of prosperity—real prosperity.

*It's sobering to contemplate how much time, effort,
sacrifice, compromise, and attention we give
to acquiring and increasing our supply of something
that is totally insignificant in eternity.*
Anne Graham Lotz

Faith-Full

Commit your works to the LORD,
and your thoughts will be established.
Proverbs 16:3 NKJV

As you take the next step in your life's journey, you should do so with hope and anticipation. After all, if you're a thoughtful woman and a thankful mother, you already have countless reasons to rejoice. But sometimes rejoicing may be the last thing on your mind. Sometimes you may fall prey to worry, frustration, anxiety, or sheer exhaustion.

The next time you become disheartened by the direction of your day or your life, ask God to help you count your blessings, not your hardships. Then commit to letting Him guide your steps through each day and through your life.

Remember that even when the challenges of the day seem daunting, God remains steadfast. And so must you.

At least ten times every day, affirm this thought:
"I expect the best and, with God's help,
will attain the best."
Norman Vincent Peale

Power Supply

*Come to Me, all of you who are weary and burdened,
and I will give you rest. All of you, take up My yoke
and learn from Me, because I am gentle and humble
in heart, and you will find rest for yourselves.
For My yoke is easy and My burden is light.*
Matthew 11:28–30 HCSB

Have you been struggling along life's road under your own power? If so, it's high time for a power boost. Are you weary, worried, or fearful? If so, it's time to turn to a strength much greater than your own.

You have, at your fingertips, a power supply that never fails: the power that flows from God. He's always willing to lend His strength to you and yours. It's up to you to realize and admit you need His help and to ask for it. When you do, He will provide it.

Some days are light and breezy, but other days require quite a bit of heavy lifting. If the weight you're carrying seems a little too heavy, don't fret. God can provide the energy you need to carry the weight. So what are you waiting for?

Life is strenuous. See that your clock does not run down.
Mrs. Charles E. Cowman

Deciding Who Rules

You shall have no other gods before Me.
Exodus 20:3 NKJV

Who rules your heart? Is it God, or is it something else? Have you given God your heart, your soul, your talents, and your time, or have you formed the unfortunate habit of giving Him little more than a few hours on Sunday morning?

In the book of Exodus, God warned that we should place no gods before Him. Yet all too often, we place our Creator in second, third, or fourth place in our lives as we worship the gods of power, money, or prestige. When we unwittingly place our quest for status above our love for the Father, we must recognize our misplaced priorities and correct our behavior.

Does God rule your heart, Mom? Make certain that the honest answer to this question is a resounding Yes! He deserves no less . . . and He loves you enough to want no less for you than the blessings you'll receive when He rules.

God made man. Man rejected God.
God won't give up until He wins him back.
Max Lucado

Stillness amid the Noise

Be still, and know that I am God.
Psalm 46:10 KJV

Are you so busy that you rush through the day with scarcely a single moment for quiet contemplation and prayer? If so, it's time to slow down and find time for that kind of stillness . . . or suffer the consequences of neglecting what your soul needs.

Our society seems to have the capacity to generate a near-infinite amount of noise. And every time somebody close by decides to crank up the volume, you may find yourself distracted, exasperated, infuriated, or all of the above. When you find your eardrums . . . and your heart . . . are left pounding, find a quiet place as quickly as possible, and bask in the silence.

Don't wait, Mom: find time today to be still and find the inner peace that accompanies silence. It's the peaceful way to live.

Never be afraid to sit awhile and think.
Lorraine Hansberry

Your Own Worst Critic

A devout life does bring wealth,
but it's the rich simplicity of being yourself before God.
1 Timothy 6:6 MSG

Are you your own worst critic? If so, maybe it's time to be a little more understanding of the woman you see when you look in the mirror.

Millions of words have been written about various ways to improve self-image and increase self-esteem. Yet maintaining a healthy self-image is, to a large extent, a matter of doing three things: (1) behaving yourself, (2) thinking healthy thoughts, and (3) finding a purpose for your life that pleases your Creator and yourself.

The Bible implies the importance of self-acceptance by teaching us to love others as we love ourselves (see Matthew 22:37–40). God accepts us just as we are. And if He accepts us—faults and all— then who are we to disagree?

Have patience with all things, but mostly with yourself.
Don't lose courage considering your own imperfections,
but instantly begin remedying them.
Every day begin the task anew.
Saint Francis de Sales

Mothers Who Keep Learning

There's something here also for seasoned men and women,
still a thing or two for the experienced to learn—
Fresh wisdom to probe and penetrate, the rhymes
and reasons of wise men and women. Start with GOD.
Proverbs 1:5–7 MSG

Even if you're a wise woman, God isn't finished with you yet. He isn't finished teaching you important lessons about life here on earth and about life eternal.

As a spiritual being you have the potential to grow in your personal knowledge of God every day you live. You can do so through prayer, through worship, through an openness to God's Spirit, and through a careful study of God's Word. Your Bible contains powerful prescriptions for everyday living. If you sincerely seek to walk with God, commit yourself to the thoughtful study of His teachings.

When you read God's Word and live according to what it says, you'll become wiser each day . . . and you'll serve as a shining example to your friends, to your family, and to the world.

If we look to God for the lesson we should learn,
we will see spiritual fruit.
Vonette Bright

November

A Thank-You Hug for Mom

Dear Mom,

The very best mothers not only give life, but they also teach it. And that's exactly what you've done. For longer than we can remember, you've taught us life's most important lessons. You are the teacher, we are the pupils, and class is still in session.

One of life's great ironies is that there's so much to learn and so little time. That's why we value the lessons you've taught us . . . and the ones you've yet to teach us.

November 1

Reason to Rejoice

*Keep your eyes focused on what is right,
and look straight ahead to what is good.*
Proverbs 4:25 NCV

As a mother you have many reasons to rejoice, starting, of course, with your kids and your family (not to mention the fact that dawn has broken on another day of life here on earth, and you're part of it). But when the demands of the day seem great, you may feel exhausted, discouraged, or both. That's when you need a fresh supply of hope . . . and God is ready, willing, and able to supply it. Your task is to ask Him for it.

Are you a mom who looks on the bright side? Hopefully you understand the importance of maintaining a positive, can-do attitude—an attitude that pleases God.

As you face the challenges of the coming day, use God's Word as a tool for directing your thoughts. When you do, your attitude will be pleasing to God, to your friends, and to yourself. And that's just one more reason to rejoice.

*No life is so hard that you can't make it easier
by the way you take it.*
Ellen Glasgow

Time to Celebrate

Weeping may endure for a night,
but joy comes in the morning.
Psalm 30:5 NKJV

Are you living a life of agitation or celebration? If you take a few moments to reflect, you'll likely agree it should be the latter. When you consider the joys and fulfillment you derive from your family, and when you stop to think about the countless blessings God has bestowed upon you and yours, you have many reasons to be celebratory.

Today celebrate the life God has given you. Put a smile on your face, kind words on your lips, and a song in your heart. Be generous with your praise and free with your encouragement. And then, with your life celebration in full swing, invite your friends to join in. After all, this is God's day, and He has commanded us to rejoice and be glad. So, with no further ado, let the celebration begin.

Be happy. It's one way of being wise.
Colette

The Loving Choice

May mercy, peace, and love be multiplied to you.
Jude 2 HCSB

Love is a choice. Either you choose to behave lovingly toward others . . . or not; either you act in ways that enhance your relationships . . . or not. But make no mistake: genuine love requires effort. Simply put, if you wish to build lasting relationships, you must be willing to do your part.

God wants more for you than mediocre relationships; He created you for far greater things. Building lasting relationships requires compassion, wisdom, empathy, kindness, courtesy, and forgiveness. If that sounds like work, it is—which is perfectly fine with God. Why? Because it's exactly the kind of work He has in mind for you, and because He knows that the fruits of your labors will enrich not just your own life but also the lives of your loved ones . . . and the lives of generations yet unborn.

Love must be learned again and again;
there is no end to it. Hate needs no instruction.
Katherine Anne Porter

Everyday Crises

*We take the good days from God—
why not also the bad days?*
Job 2:10 MSG

You live in a world that seeks to snare your attention and lead you away from your loving, heavenly Father. So each time you're tempted to distance yourself from God, you face a spiritual crisis. A few of these crises may be monumental in scope, but most will be the small, everyday variety. In fact, life can be seen as one test after another—and with each crisis comes yet another opportunity to grow closer to God . . . or to distance yourself from Him and His wonderful plan for your life.

Today, Mom, you will face many opportunities to say yes to your Creator—and you'll also find plenty of opportunities to say no to Him. Your answers will determine whether you're moving toward or away from the One who made you and loves you. So in each of these crises, whether huge or tiny . . . answer carefully.

*Crisis brings us face to face with our inadequacy,
and our inadequacy in turn leads us
to the inexhaustible sufficiency of God.*
Catherine Marshall

When Faith Slips Away

*Immediately the father of the child cried out
and said with tears, "Lord, I believe; help my unbelief!"*
Mark 9:24 NKJV

Sometimes we feel threatened by the storms of life. During these moments, when our hearts are flooded with uncertainty, we must remember that God is not simply near; He is here, right by our side.

Have you ever felt your faith in God slipping away? If so, you're in good company. Even the most faithful moms occasionally find themselves in a battle with discouragement and doubt. But even when you feel far removed from God, God never leaves your side. He is always with you, always willing to calm the storms of life. When you sincerely seek His presence—when you genuinely try to establish a deeper, more meaningful relationship with Him—God will calm your fears, answer your prayers, and restore your soul.

*We are most vulnerable to the piercing winds of doubt
when we distance ourselves from the mission and
fellowship to which Christ has called us.*
Joni Eareckson Tada

Caring for Aging Parents

*Let them first learn to do their duty to their own family
and to repay their parents or grandparents.
That pleases God.*
1 Timothy 5:4 NCV

If you're responsible, either directly or indirectly, for the care of aging parents, you already know that it's a challenging job. But you also know that caring for your loved ones is not simply a duty; it's also a responsibility—and a privilege.

Caring for an elderly adult requires a mixture of diplomacy, patience, insight, perseverance, gentleness, strength, compassion, wisdom, empathy, and, most of all, an endless supply of love. That's no small challenge.

Sometimes the job of caring for aging parents may seem to be a thankless task, but it's not really. Even if your parents don't fully appreciate your sacrifices, God does. And of this you may be certain: your heavenly Father will find surprising ways to reward your faithfulness . . . now and in heaven.

*There is no friendship, no love,
like that of the parent and the child.*
Henry Ward Beecher

Focusing on Fitness

*Didn't you realize that your body is a sacred place,
the place of the Holy Spirit? Don't you see that you can't
live however you please, squandering what God paid such
a high price for? The physical part of you is not some piece
of property belonging to the spiritual part of you.*

1 Corinthians 6:19 MSG

Physical fitness requires discipline: the discipline to exercise regularly and the discipline to eat sensibly—it's as simple as that. But here's the catch: while understanding the need for discipline is easy, leading a disciplined life is hard for must of us. Why? Because it's usually more fun to eat a second piece of cake than it is to jog a second lap around the track. Yet as we survey the second helpings that all too often find their way onto our plates, we should consider this: when we behave in undisciplined ways, we're the ones who inevitably suffer.

Are you choosing to treat your body like a temple, Mom? Hopefully so, because physical fitness has a lot to do with how well you live and how long you live. So treat your body like a one-of-a-kind gift from God . . . because that's precisely what your body is.

*The soul is the user, the body for use;
hence the one is master, the other servant.*

Saint Ambrose

Relationships According to God

*Regarding life together and getting along with each other,
you don't need me to tell you what to do.
You're God-taught in these matters. Just love one another!*
1 Thessalonians 4:9 MSG

As we travel along life's road, we build lifelong relationships with a small circle of dear family and friends. Well, Mom, one important way to build and maintain healthy relationships is by following the advice that can be found in God's instruction manual (also known as the Bible).

Healthy relationships are built on honesty, compassion, responsible behavior, and trust. Healthy relationships are built on the Golden Rule. Healthy relationships are built on sharing and caring. All of these principles are taught time and time again in God's Word.

When we read the Bible and its instructions, we enrich our own lives and the lives of those closest to us. So next time you're wondering how to act toward a friend or family member, pull out your Bible and start reading. The answers you need can be found there; your job is to apply them to your relationships.

*You will accomplish more by kind words
and a courteous manner than by anger and sharp rebuke,
which should never be used, except in necessity.*
Saint Angela Merici

Marveling at the Miracle of Nature

When I look at the night sky and see the work of your
fingers—the moon and the stars you have set in place—
what are mortals that you should think of us,
mere humans that you should care for us?
Psalm 8:3–4 NLT

When we consider God's glorious universe, we marvel at the miracle of nature. The smallest seedlings and grandest stars are all part of God's infinite creation. God has placed His handiwork on display for all to see, and if we're wise, we'll make a little time each day to celebrate the world that surrounds us.

Today, Mom, as you fulfill the demands of your busy life, pause to consider the majesty of heaven and earth. It's as miraculous as it is beautiful, as incomprehensible as it is breathtaking.

Psalm 19 reminds us that the heavens are a declaration of God's glory. May we never cease to praise our heavenly Father for a universe that stands as an awesome testimony to His presence and His power.

Go outside, to the fields, enjoy nature and the sunshine,
go out and try to recapture happiness in yourself
and in God. Think of all the beauty that's still left
in and around you and be happy!
Anne Frank

The Size of God's Love

*God is love, and the one who remains in love
remains in God, and God remains in him.*
1 John 4:16 HCSB

God is love—it's a broad and sweeping statement, and it's a profoundly important description of who God is and how God works. God's love is perfect. When we open our hearts to Him, we're touched by the Creator's hand, and we are transformed.

Sometimes we don't spend much time thinking about God or His love. Instead, we focus on the obligations and distractions of everyday living. But if we pause to compare the size of our problems to the size of God's love, we'll be comforted.

So today, Mom, even if you can only carve out a few quiet moments, use those minutes to talk with God and to offer prayers of sincere thanks to your Father for His marvelous, limitless love.

*Love has its source in God,
for love is the very essence of His being.*
Kay Arthur

Still Growing

*When I was a child, I spoke and thought
and reasoned as a child does. But when I grew up,
I put away childish things.*
1 Corinthians 13:11 NLT

Every new day presents opportunities for emotional and spiritual growth. We can, if we choose, be continually transformed—moment by moment and day by day—into more mature, thoughtful adults. How? A good way to start is by putting away "childish things."

Young children can be easily overwhelmed by feelings of anger, envy, selfishness, or frustration. But as adults we possess stronger emotional defenses against these sorts of negative feelings. And if we're wise, we'll do our best to distance ourselves from childish emotions and behaviors that interfere with our spiritual health and spiritual growth.

So, Mom, here's something to think about: what childish thing will you put away today? And what sort of blessings—spiritual, emotional, or otherwise—can you expect to receive when you do?

*If I long to improve my brother,
the first step toward doing so is to improve myself.*
Christina Rossetti

Sad Days

*This is what the LORD Almighty says: Once again old men
and women will walk Jerusalem's streets with a cane
and sit together in the city squares. And the streets
of the city will be filled with boys and girls at play.*
Zechariah 8:4–5 NLT

Some days are light and happy, and some days are
not. When we face the inevitable dark days of life,
we must choose how we will respond. Will we allow
ourselves to sink even deeper into our own sadness, or
will we do the difficult work of pulling ourselves out?
We can bring light to the dark days of life by turning
first to God, and then to trusted family members and
friends. Then we must go to work helping to solve the
problems that confront us. When we do, the clouds
will eventually part, and the sun will shine once more
upon our souls.

So the next time you face one of those days when
your emotions are flatter than a pancake, try this: pray
for God's strength, share your burdens with people
you trust, and do something constructive. When you
do, you won't stay down for long.

*It is not what they take away from you that counts.
It's what you do with what you have left.*
Hubert H. Humphrey

Pity Parties

*He did not many mighty works there
because of their unbelief.*
Matthew 13:58 KJV

Have you ever invited yourself to a pity party? If so, you'll probably agree that you would have been better off sending your regrets.

Self-pity is not only an unproductive way to think, it's also an affront to your Father in heaven. Self-pity and thanksgiving cannot coexist in the same mind. Bitterness and joy cannot coexist in the same heart. Gratitude and despair are mutually exclusive.

So, Mom, if you're allowing pain and worry to dominate your life, train yourself to think less about your troubles and more about God's blessings. After all, hasn't He given you enough blessings to occupy your thoughts all day, every day, from now through all eternity? Of course He has! So focus your thoughts on Him, and let your worries fend for themselves.

*Self-pity is our worst enemy, and if we yield to it,
we can never do anything wise in the world.*
Helen Keller

Doing What's Right

*Follow the whole instruction the LORD your God
has commanded you, so that you may live,
prosper, and have a long life.*
Deuteronomy 5:33 HCSB

As loving mothers we must teach our children to obey the rules of society and the laws of God. God's laws are contained in a guidebook for right living called the Bible. It contains thorough instructions which, if followed, lead to fulfillment and peace. But when we choose to ignore God's commandments, for whatever reason, the results are as predictable as they are tragic.

Talking about obedience is easy; living obediently is considerably harder. But if we are to be responsible role models for our families and friends, we must study God's Word and obey it.

So today, Mom, as you consider the lessons you intend to teach your children (or your children's children), remember to stress the importance of doing what's right. It's a lesson that never goes out of fashion.

*God asked both Noah and Joshua to do something
unusual and difficult. They did it, and their obedience
brought them deliverance.*
Mary Morrison Suggs

The Practice of Praise

*Through Jesus let us always offer to God our sacrifice
of praise, coming from lips that speak his name.*
Hebrews 13:15 NCV

God certainly deserves our praise—not just for the blessings He's given us but simply for who He is. But sometimes we allow ourselves to become so preoccupied with our everyday lives that we forget to say thank you to the Giver of all good gifts.

Worship and praise should be a part of everything we do. Otherwise, we quickly lose perspective on life as we fall prey to the demands of the moment.

Do you sincerely desire to be a faithful follower of the God who has given you a loving family, eternal love, and eternal life? Of course you do! So praise Him for who He is and for what He has done for you and yours. And one more thing, Mom: don't just praise Him on Sunday morning; praise Him all day long, every day, for as long as you live . . . and then for all eternity.

*Praising God reduces your cares, levels your anxieties,
and multiplies your blessings.*
Suzanne Dale Ezell

Embracing Every Stage of Life

*Youth may be admired for vigor,
but gray hair gives prestige to old age.*
Proverbs 20:29 MSG

We live in a society that glorifies youth. The messages we receive through most media are unrelenting. We're told we must do everything in our power to retain a youthful mind-set and a youthful appearance. The goal, we are told (at least implicitly), is to remain forever young. Yet this goal is not only unrealistic, it's also unworthy of women who understand what true beauty is—and what it isn't.

When it comes to health and beauty, wise women focus more on health than on beauty. In fact, when you take care of your physical, spiritual, and mental health, your appearance will tend to take care of itself. Even so, no matter what we do, outside beauty is fleeting. But remember: God loves you during every stage of life, Mom. So embrace the aging process for what it is—an opportunity to grow wiser . . . and closer to your loved ones and to your Creator.

*There is a fountain of youth. It is your mind,
your talents, the creativity you bring to your life
and the lives of people you love.*
Sophia Loren

Purpose Day by Day

*Yet Lord, You are our Father; we are the clay,
and You are our potter; we all are the work of Your hands.*

Isaiah 64:8 HCSB

Each morning, as the sun rises, you welcome a new day—one that is filled to the brim with opportunities, with possibilities, and with God's presence. As you contemplate God's blessings in your own life, it's important that you prayerfully seek His guidance for the day ahead.

Discovering God's purpose for your life is a daily journey, one that should be guided by the teachings of God's Word. As you reflect upon God's promises and upon the meaning those promises hold for you and your family, ask God to lead you throughout the coming day. Let your heavenly Father direct your steps; concentrate on what God wants you to do now, and leave the distant future in hands that are far more capable than your own: His hands.

You're the only one who can do what you do.

Lois Evans

Beyond the Comfort Zone

Be not afraid, only believe.
Mark 5:36 KJV

Risk is an unavoidable fact of life. From the moment we rise in the morning until the moment we drift off to sleep at night, we face a wide array of risks, both great and small.

Some risks, of course, should be avoided at all costs—these include risky behaviors that drive us further and further away from God's will for our lives. Yet other risks—the kind we must take in order to expand our horizons and our faith—should be accepted as the price we pay for living full and productive lives.

Have you planted yourself firmly inside your own comfort zone? If so, maybe it's time to reconsider the direction and scope of your activities. God has big plans for you, but those plans will most likely require you to step outside of your comfort zone. But don't be afraid. Believe. Because each step is one God will take with you.

If I'm not free to fail, I'm not free to take risks.
And everything in life that's worth doing involves
a willingness to take a risk and involves the risk of failure.
I have to try, but I do not have to succeed.
Madeleine L'Engle

Wise Words

From a wise mind comes wise speech;
the words of the wise are persuasive.
Proverbs 16:23 NLT

How important are the words we speak? More important than we may realize. Our words echo beyond place and time. If our words are encouraging, we can lift others up; if our words are hurtful, we can drag others down.

So, Mom, here are some questions for you and your family to consider: Do you really try to be a source of encouragement to the people you encounter every day? Are you careful to speak words that lift those people up?

If that's how you want to use your words, you'll learn to avoid angry outbursts. You'll refrain from impulsive outpourings. And you'll terminate tantrums. Instead, you will speak words of encouragement and hope to friends, to family members, to coworkers, and even to strangers.

By the way, all the aforementioned people have at least one thing in common: they, like just about everybody else in the world, need all the hope and encouragement they can get. Offer them some today with your wisely chosen words.

Kind words can be short and easy to speak,
but their echoes are truly endless.
Mother Teresa

What We Become

It is God who is working in you,
enabling you both to will and to act for His good purpose.
Philippians 2:13 HCSB

The old saying is both familiar and true: what we are is God's gift to us; what we become is our gift to God. Each of us possesses special talents, given by God, that can be nurtured or ignored. Our challenge is to nurture them and help them to grow—to use our abilities to the greatest extent possible and to use them in ways that honor our Savior.

Are you using your talents to make God's world a better place? If so, keep up the good work! But if you have gifts that you haven't fully explored and developed, perhaps you need to have a chat with the Creator who gave you those gifts in the first place. Your talents are priceless treasures from your heavenly Father. Don't neglect them; use them. After all, Mom, one of the best ways to say thank you for a gift is to use it.

Employ whatever God has entrusted you with,
in doing good, all possible good,
in every possible kind and degree.
John Wesley

Building Ties That Bind

The world with its lust is passing away,
but the one who does God's will remains forever.
1 John 2:17 HCSB

It takes time to build strong family ties . . . lots of time. Yet we live in a world where time seems to be an ever-shrinking commodity as we rush from place to place with seldom a moment to spare.

Has the busy pace of life robbed you of sufficient time with your loved ones? If so, it's time to fine-tune your schedule . . . and your priorities. And God can help.

When you make God a full partner in every aspect of your life, He will lead you along the proper path: His path. When you allow God to reign supreme in your life, He will enrich your relationships. So as you plan for the day ahead, make God's priorities your priorities. When you do, you'll be amazed at how well everything else falls neatly into place.

Time isn't a commodity, something you pass around
like cake. Time is the substance of life.
When anyone asks you to give your time,
they're really asking for a chunk of your life.
Antoinette Bosco

Eternal Wisdom

*Happy is the person who finds wisdom
and gains understanding.*
Proverbs 3:13 NLT

Here in the twenty-first century, commentary is commonplace and information is everywhere. But the ultimate source of wisdom, the kind of timeless wisdom God willingly shares with His children, is still available from a unique source: the Bible.

The wisdom of the world changes with the ever-shifting sands of public opinion. God's wisdom does not. His wisdom is eternal. It never changes. And it most certainly is the wisdom that you, as a thinking mother, should use to plan your day and your life.

Your Bible is an invaluable asset for building a better life, a stronger faith, and a closer family. So the best day to begin seriously contemplating God's message is always this day. Don't wait a minute longer!

A Bible in the hand is worth two in the bookcase.
Source Unknown

Where to Take Your Worries

Seek first his kingdom and his righteousness, and all these things will be given to you as well. Therefore do not worry about tomorrow, for tomorrow will worry about itself. Each day has enough trouble of its own.
Matthew 6:33–34 NIV

If you're like most moms, on occasion you find yourself worrying about health, about finances, about safety, about relationships, about family, and about countless other challenges in life, some great and some small. Where's the best place to take your worries? Take them to God. And after you've talked to your Counselor, it also helps to talk openly to the people who love you, the trusted friends and family members who know you best. The more you talk—and the more you pray—the better you'll feel.

So instead of worrying about tomorrow, do today's work and leave the rest up to God. You'll discover that if you do your part today, God will take care of today and the future too.

Today is mine. Tomorrow is none of my business.
If I peer anxiously into the fog of the future,
I will strain my spiritual eyes so that I will not see clearly what is required of me now.
Elisabeth Elliot

Accepting the Past

One thing I do: Forgetting what is behind
and straining toward what is ahead,
I press on toward the goal to win the prize for which
God has called me heavenward in Christ Jesus.
Philippians 3:13–14 NIV

Can you find the courage to accept the past by forgiving all those who have injured you—and by forgiving yourself? If you can, you'll be able to look to the future with a sense of optimism and hope.

God has instructed us to place our hopes in Him, and He has promised that we will be His throughout eternity. Your job, Mom, is to take God at His Word and to accept His invitation.

We all face occasional disappointments and failures while we're here on earth, but these are only temporary defeats. This world can be a place of trials and tribulations, yet we are secure when we trust God. He has promised us peace, joy, and eternal life if we'll follow Him. And God keeps His promises—today, tomorrow, and forever.

*The life you have led doesn't need to be
the only life you'll have.*
Anna Quindlen

Hope Today

Full of hope, you'll relax, confident again;
you'll look around, sit back, and take it easy.
Job 11:18 MSG

Are you a hope-filled mom? You should be. After all, God is good; His love endures; and He has blessed you with a loving family. But sometimes, in life's darker moments, it's easy to lose sight of those blessings. And when you do, it's easy to lose hope.

If hope ever becomes a scarce commodity around your house, or if you find yourself falling into the spiritual traps of worry and discouragement, turn your concerns over to God in prayer. Then seek wisdom and encouragement from trusted friends and family members. And remember this: the world can be a place of difficulty, but God's love conquers all; He will bring you peace, joy, and eternal life. And when you believe His promises, you'll find hope for today . . . and every day.

Hope is the feeling you have that the feeling
you have isn't permanent.
Jean Kerr

Accepting God's Abundance

*I have come that they may have life,
and that they may have it more abundantly.*
John 10:10 NKJV

The Bible promises that we may enjoy God's abundance. But every mother knows that some days are so busy and so hurried that abundance of anything but work seems only a distant promise. It's not. You can claim God's abundance every day—and you should.

Do you desire God's blessings for yourself and your family? Of course you do. And it's worth remembering that God's rewards are available to you and yours. These rewards may have little to do with material possessions. Most of them are spiritual rewards that extend beyond the temporal boundaries of this world.

Everlasting abundance is available to all those who claim it, including you. May you and your family members claim these riches—and may you share them—beginning today.

*God's riches are beyond anything we could ask
or even dare to imagine! If my life gets gooey and stale,
I have no excuse.*
Barbara Johnson

Turning Away from Anger

*When you are angry, do not sin,
and be sure to stop being angry before the end of the day.
Do not give the devil a way to defeat you.*
Ephesians 4:26–27 NCV

Perhaps God gave each of us one mouth and two ears in order that we might listen twice as much as we speak. Unfortunately, many of us do the opposite—especially when we become angry.

Sometime today (or many times) you may be tempted to strike out in anger at a family member, a friend, or even a complete stranger. Don't do it! When you start to lose your temper over the minor inconveniences of life, or even the major upsets, take a deep breath and do the hard (and wise) thing: control your temper before your tempter controls you.

As the old saying goes, "Anger usually improves nothing but the arch of a cat's back." So don't allow anger to rule your life—or even your day. Life is simply too short to waste your time and energy being angry.

He who angers you conquers you.
Sister Elizabeth Kenny

Serenity

*Those who love your law have great peace
and do not stumble.*
Psalm 119:165 NLT

American theologian Reinhold Niebuhr composed a profoundly simple verse that came to be known as the Serenity Prayer: "God, grant me the serenity to accept the things I cannot change, courage to change the things I can, and the wisdom to know the difference." Niebuhr's words are far easier for most of us to recite than they are to live by. Why? Because most of us want life to unfold according to our own wishes. We don't want to have to accept things we don't like or do the work required to make changes. But sometimes God has plans for us and for our families that involve both.

When you trust God, you can be comforted in the knowledge that your Creator is both loving and wise. And His plans are always for your benefit, Mom. So offer up a sincere Serenity Prayer, and enjoy the peace that comes when you remember that God understands His plans perfectly well, even when you do not.

*Once the "what" is decided, the "how" always follows.
We must not make the "how" an excuse
for not facing and accepting the "what."*
Pearl S. Buck

Beyond Broken Dreams

Those who trust in the LORD are like Mount Zion.
It cannot be shaken; it remains forever.
Psalm 125:1 HCSB

Some of our most important dreams are the ones we abandon. Some of our most important goals are the ones we don't attain. Sometimes our most important journeys are the ones we take to the winding conclusions of what seem to be dead ends. Thankfully, with God there are no dead ends; there are only opportunities to learn, to yield, to trust, to serve, and to grow.

The next time you experience one of life's disappointments, don't despair—and don't be afraid to try Plan B. View every setback as an opportunity to choose a different, more fitting path. Consider that God may be leading you in an entirely different direction, a direction of His choosing. And as you take your next step, Mom, have faith that what looks to you like a dead end may, in fact, be the fast lane according to God.

Just remember, every flower that ever bloomed
had to go through a whole lot of dirt to get there!
Barbara Johnson

A Guilty Conscience

*Let us come near to God with a sincere heart
and a sure faith, because we have been made free
from a guilty conscience, and our bodies have been
washed with pure water.*

Hebrews 10:22 NCV

It has been said that character is what we are when nobody's watching. How true. When we do things that we know aren't right, we often try to hide them from our families and friends. But even then, God is watching.

Few things in life torment us more than a guilty conscience. And few things in life provide more contentment than the knowledge that we have a clean conscience through God's grace and our faithfulness to Him.

If you sincerely want to create the best possible life for yourself and your loved ones, never ignore your God-given conscience. And remember this: when you walk with God, you won't need to look over your shoulder to see who, besides God, is watching.

*One thing that can't abide by majority rule
is a person's conscience.*

Harper Lee

December

A Thank-You Hug for Mom

Dear Mom,

As the Christmas season rolls around yet again, we thank you for holidays past—for all the things you did to fill those memory-making moments with laughter and excitement. Holidays, it seems, have a way of getting out of control; but even on the days when you were overworked and overstressed, you kept your holiday spirit. We noticed . . . and we'll never forget.

Making Better Decisions

If you need wisdom—if you want to know what
God wants you to do—ask him, and he will gladly tell you.
He will not resent your asking.
James 1:5 NLT

From the instant you wake in the morning until the moment you nod off to sleep at night, you make countless decisions: decisions about the things you do, decisions about the words you speak, and decisions about the thoughts you think. Simply put, the quality of those decisions will determine, to a large extent, the quality of your life.

Are you willing to invest the time, the effort, and the prayers needed to make wise decisions? Are you willing to take your concerns to God and to avail yourself of the messages and mentors He has placed along your path? If you're willing to start, Mom, you'll find that you also start making better decisions . . . and reaping the rewards of wise living.

As we trust God to give us wisdom for today's decisions,
He will lead us a step at a time into what
He wants us to be doing in the future.
Theodore Epp

December 2

Big Dreams

It is pleasant to see dreams come true.
Proverbs 13:19 NLT

It takes courage to dream big dreams for yourself and your family. But you can discover the courage to dream big when you do three things: accept the past, trust God to handle the future, and make the most of the time He has given you today.

Are you excited about the opportunities of today and thrilled by the possibilities of tomorrow? Do you confidently expect God to lead you and yours to a place of abundance, peace, and joy? If you trust God's promises, you can have faith that your future is intensely and eternally bright.

Today promise yourself that you'll do your family (and the world) a king-sized favor by wholeheartedly pursuing your dreams. After all, no dreams are too big for God. So start living—and dreaming—accordingly.

Far away in the sunshine are my highest aspirations.
I may not reach them, but I can look up
and see the beauty, believe in them,
and try to follow where they lead.
Louisa May Alcott

Faith and Wholeness

The just shall live by faith.
Hebrews 10:38 NKJV

A suffering woman sought healing in an unusual way: she simply touched the hem of Jesus's garment. When she did, Jesus turned and said, "Daughter, be of good comfort; thy faith hath made thee whole" (Matthew 9:22 KJV). We, too, can be made whole when we place our faith completely and unwaveringly in God.

As you learn to trust God more and more, you'll be amazed at the marvelous things He can do with you and through you. So strengthen your faith through worship, through Bible study, and through prayer. Then trust God's plans. Your heavenly Father is standing at the door of your heart. If you reach out to Him in faith, He will give you peace and heal your broken spirit. Be bold enough to touch even the smallest fragment of the Master's garment, and He will make you whole.

Let me encourage you to continue to wait with faith.
God may not perform a miracle,
but He is trustworthy to touch you and make you whole
where there used to be a hole.
Lisa Whelchel

The Rule That's Golden

This royal law is found in the Scriptures:
"Love your neighbor as you love yourself."
If you obey this law, then you are doing right.
James 2:8 ICB

Is the Golden Rule one of the rules that governs your household? Hopefully so. Obeying it is a sure way to improve all your relationships, including your relationships with the people who happen to live in your home. But the reverse is also true: if you or your loved ones ignore the Golden Rule, you're headed for trouble, and fast.

God's Word makes it clear: we are to treat others with respect, kindness, fairness, and courtesy. And He knows we can do so if we try, and with His help—which He stands ready to give.

So, Mom, as you fulfill your many obligations, weave the thread of kindness into the fabric of your day. When you do, everybody wins . . . especially you.

All our goodness is a loan; God is the owner.
Saint John of the Cross

Small Choices

Not my will, but thine, be done.
Luke 22:42 KJV

Each of us faces thousands of small choices each day, choices that make up the fabric of daily life. When we align those choices with God's commandments, and when we align our lives with God's will, we'll receive His blessings in abundance. But when we struggle against God's will for our lives—when we insist on doing things our way, not His way—we'll reap a less bountiful harvest.

Today you'll make thousands of small choices; as you do, use God's Word as your guide. And while you're at it, Mom, pay careful attention to the small, quiet voice—your conscience—that God has placed in your heart. In matters great and small, seek God's will and trust Him. He will never lead you astray.

Joy is not gush; joy is not mere jolliness.
Joy is perfect acquiescence, acceptance,
and rest in God's will, whatever comes.
Amy Carmichael

Gentleness of Spirit

*Your beauty should not come from outward adornment,
such as braided hair and the wearing of gold jewelry and
fine clothes. Instead, it should be that of your inner self,
the unfading beauty of a gentle and quiet spirit,
which is of great worth in God's sight.*

1 Peter 3:3–4 NIV

At times it's difficult to be gentle. As frail human beings, we're subject to the normal frustrations of daily life, and when they overwhelm us, we're tempted to strike out in anger.

As long as you live, Mom, you will face countless opportunities to lose your temper over relatively little things: a traffic jam, a spilled cup of coffee, an inconsiderate comment, a broken promise. But don't do it. Turn away from anger, and turn instead to your heavenly Father. When you do, you'll discover that God can restore your sense of peace and perspective, and He can fill you with a loving spirit that will help you deal gently and generously with others.

*This hard place in which you perhaps find yourself
is the very place in which God is giving you opportunity
to look only to Him, to spend time in prayer, and to learn
long-suffering, gentleness, meekness—in short, to learn
the depths of the love that Christ Himself
has poured out on all of us.*

Elisabeth Elliot

Protected by the Hand of God

*Whatever is born of God overcomes the world.
And this is the victory that has overcome
the world—our faith.*

1 John 5:4 NKJV

Have you ever faced challenges that seemed too huge to handle? Have you ever encountered big problems that, despite your best efforts, you simply couldn't solve? If so, you know how uncomfortable it is to feel helpless in the face of difficult circumstances. Thankfully, even when there's nowhere else to turn, you can turn to God. When you pray to Him, He will respond.

God's hand uplifts those who turn their hearts to Him. Count yourself among that number. When you do, you can live courageously and joyfully, knowing that all these problems will pass—but that God's love for you will not. And then, Mom, you can draw strength from the knowledge that you are a marvelous creation, loved and protected by the ever-present hand of God.

*Worries carry responsibilities that belong to God,
not to you. Worry does not enable us to escape evil;
it makes us unfit to cope with it when it comes.*

Corrie ten Boom

God's Gift to You

*Everything God made is good, and nothing should be
refused if it is accepted with thanks.*
1 Timothy 4:4 NCV

Life is God's gift to you, and He intends that you
celebrate His glorious gift. So when, precisely,
will your celebration begin? If you're a mom who
communicates with your Creator and treasures each
day, the answer to that question should be, "As soon
as possible, if not sooner!"

Folks who choose to let their days be centered on
God's love and God's promises are, quite literally,
transformed: they see the world differently, they act
differently, and they feel differently about themselves,
their families, and their neighbors.

So, Mom, whatever this day holds for you, begin
it and end it with God. And throughout the day, give
thanks for His wondrous gift of life. God's love for
you is infinite. Accept it joyously and be thankful.

*Life is not a problem to be solved;
it is an adventure to be lived.*
John Eldredge

The Wisdom to Be Humble

Don't be selfish. . . . Be humble,
thinking of others as better than yourself.
Philippians 2:3 TLB

Humility is not, in most cases, a naturally occurring human trait. Most of us seem more than willing to overestimate the importance of our own accomplishments. We're tempted to say, "Look how wonderful I am!" hoping all the world will agree with our self-appraisals. But those of us who fall prey to pride should beware—God is definitely not impressed by our boasting.

God honors humility . . . and He rewards those who humbly serve Him. So, Mom, if you've not yet overcome the tendency to overestimate your importance, God has some important lessons to teach you—lessons about humility that you still need to learn. And the sooner you learn those lessons, the happier you'll be.

We are never stronger than the moment
we admit we are weak.
Beth Moore

Laughing with Life

Laugh with your happy friends when they're happy.
Romans 12:15 MSG

Every relationship, whether it's with your spouse, your kids, or your coworkers, can (and should) be seasoned with good, clean fun. But sometimes, instead of viewing our world with a mixture of optimism and humor, we allow worries and distractions to rob us of the joy God wants us to experience.

If you're weighed down by the demands of parenting, you know all too well that a good laugh can be hard to find. But it need not be so. If you're having trouble getting your funny bone in gear, here's a helpful hint: lighten up and don't take things so seriously (especially yourself)! Everything feels better (and usually goes more smoothly) when you learn to laugh at yourself and when you learn to find humor in life's little mishaps.

Your life is either a comedy or a tragedy, depending upon how you look at it. Make yours a comedy.

Laughter is, by definition, healthy.
Doris Lessing

Good Deeds

A good person produces good deeds from a good heart.
Luke 6:45 NLT

Abigail Adams was married to U.S. president John Adams for fifty-four years, and when their son John Quincy Adams was elected to the highest office in the land, she became the first woman to be both the wife and the mother of U.S. presidents. Yet this wife and mother of remarkable men had some remarkable insight of her own: she warned, "We have too many high sounding words, and too few actions that correspond with them." Her words remind us of the need to do, not just talk about doing, the right thing.

Chances are you're capable of much more than you realize. So if you'd like to jump-start your life, try Abigail's formula for success: use a little less talk and a little more action. Because it doesn't take a founding mother to know that millions of good intentions pale in comparison to a single good deed.

You must do the thing you think you cannot do.
Eleanor Roosevelt

When You're Feeling Blue

Though I sit in darkness, the Lord will be my light.
Micah 7:8 HCSB

The sadness that accompanies any significant loss is a fact of life. In time, sadness runs its course and gradually abates. Depression, on the other hand, is a physical and emotional condition that can last for years—yet it doesn't have to. Today depression is highly treatable.

If you find yourself feeling blue, perhaps it's a reasonable reaction to the ups and downs of daily life. But if you or someone close to you has become clinically depressed, it's time to seek professional help.

We must choose how we will respond when we're hurting. Will we allow ourselves to sink even more deeply into sadness, or will we do the difficult work of pulling ourselves out—even if that simply means asking for help? We can bring light to the dark days of life by turning first to God, and then to trusted family members, friends, and medical professionals. When we seek help from the right sources, the clouds will eventually part, and the sun will shine once more upon our souls.

Never give way to melancholy; resist it steadily,
for the habit will encroach.
Sydney Smith

The Wisdom to Persevere

Be strong and do not give up,
for your work will be rewarded.
2 Chronicles 15:7 NIV

Ask almost any successful mom about the ups
and downs of family life, and she'll tell you
that occasional disappointments and failures are
inevitable. Those setbacks, false starts, and roadblocks
are simply the side effects of our willingness to take
risks in order to follow our dreams. But even when
we come face to face with failure, we must never lose
faith.

Are you willing to keep fighting the good
fight, even when you've encountered unexpected
difficulties? Have you determined to encourage your
children to do the same? If so, you and yours may
soon be surprised at the creative ways God finds to
help determined people . . . people like you . . . who
possess the wisdom and the courage to persevere.

Failure is one of life's most powerful teachers.
How we handle our failures determines whether
we're going to simply "get by" in life or "press on."
Beth Moore

Your Potential

*Have faith in the LORD your God, and you will stand
strong. Have faith in his prophets, and you will succeed.*
2 Chronicles 20:20 NCV

Have you thought much lately about your potential, Mom? Do you expect your future to be bright? Are you willing to dream . . . and are you willing to work hard to make your dreams a reality? Hopefully so—after all, God's Word tells us that we can do "all things" through Him (Philippians 4:13 NASB). Yet most of us live far below our potential. We take half measures; we dream small dreams; we waste precious time and energy on the distractions of the world. But God has bigger, better plans for us.

God wants us to move mountains, not reposition molehills. And if we ask God, He'll give us the strength and the courage to move those mountains, starting now.

You and your loved ones possess great potential, potential that you must pursue or forfeit. Begin pursuing God's best for you today.

*God created us with an overwhelming desire to soar.
He designed us to be tremendously productive and
"to mount up with wings like eagles," realistically
dreaming of what He can do with our potential.*
Carol Kent

In Focus

*Summing it all up, friends, I'd say you'll do best by
filling your minds and meditating on things true, noble,
reputable, authentic, compelling, gracious—the best,
not the worst; the beautiful, not the ugly; things to praise,
not things to curse. Put into practice what you learned
from me, what you heard and saw and realized.
Do that, and God, who makes everything work together,
will work you into his most excellent harmonies.*
Philippians 4:8–9 MSG

Where is your focus today, Mom? Are you willing to focus your thoughts and energies on God's blessings and on His will for your life? Or will you turn your thoughts to other things? This day—and every day—is a chance to celebrate the life God has given you. To give thanks to the one who has offered you more blessings than you can possibly count.

Today, why not focus on the positive aspects of your life? Why not take time to celebrate God's glorious creation? Why not act according to your hopes instead of your fears? When you think optimistically about yourself and your world, you can then share your optimism with others. They'll be better for it, of course . . . but the biggest winner will be you.

Whatever we focus on determines what we become.
E. Stanley Jones

Keeping Up

*Our only goal is to please God
whether we live here or there.*
2 Corinthians 5:9 NCV

As a member of this highly competitive, twenty-first-century world, you know that the demands and expectations of everyday living can seem burdensome, even overwhelming, at times. Keeping up with the Joneses can become a full-time job if you let it. But a better strategy would be to stop trying to impress the neighbors and to concentrate, instead, on pleasing God.

Perhaps you have high aspirations for yourself and your family; if so, congratulations! You're willing to dream big, and that's a good thing. But as you consider your life's purpose, don't allow your quest for earthly excellence to interfere with the spiritual journey God has planned for you.

Whom will you try to please today, Mom—your neighbor or your Creator?

*Keeping up with the Joneses is like keeping up
with a scared jackrabbit—only harder.*
Marie T. Freeman

The Heart of a Servant

The one who blesses others is abundantly blessed;
those who help others are helped.
Proverbs 11:25 MSG

Mom, do you consider each day a glorious opportunity to improve your little corner of the world? Hopefully so, because your corner of the world, like so many other corners of the world, can use all the help it can get.

You can make a difference—a big difference—in the quality of your own life and the lives of your family, your neighbors, your friends, and your community. You make the world a better place whenever you find a need and fill it. And in these difficult days, the needs are great—but so is your ability to meet those needs.

So as you plan the day ahead, be sure to make time for service. And then expect good things to happen as God richly rewards your generosity.

My heart's desire is to find more opportunities
to give myself away and teach my children
the joy of service at the same time.
Liz Curtis Higgs

Depending on God

Whoever calls on the name of the LORD will be delivered.
Joel 2:32 NASB

God is a never-ending source of strength and courage for those who call on Him. When we're weary, He gives us strength. When we see no hope, God reminds us of His promises. When we grieve, God wipes away our tears.

Do you feel overwhelmed by the responsibilities of motherhood? Do you feel pressured by the ever-increasing demands of your family, your friends, and your career? If so, then turn your concerns over to God in prayer. He knows your needs, and He has promised to meet those needs. Whatever your circumstances, God will protect you and care for you . . . if you let Him. Get to know Him better today, and allow Him to renew your spirit and your strength. When you trust Him and Him alone, He will never fail you.

When we reach the end of our strength, wisdom, and personal resources, we enter into the beginning of His glorious provisions.
Patsy Clairmont

Busy with Our Thoughts

*People's thoughts can be like a deep well,
but someone with understanding
can find the wisdom there.*
Proverbs 20:5 NCV

We humans are always busy with our thoughts. We simply can't help ourselves. Our brains never shut off: even while we're sleeping, we mull things over in our minds. The question is not if we will think; the question is how will we think and what will we think about.

Today, Mom, focus your thoughts on God: on His plan and His love. And if you've been plagued by pessimism and doubt, it's time to turn that troubled thinking around. Place your faith in God and give thanks for His blessings. Think about your world, your family, and your life from a foundation of hope. It's the wisest way to use your mind. And besides, since you'll always be busy with your thoughts, you might as well make those thoughts pleasing (to God and you) and helpful (to you and yours).

*No matter how little we can change about
our circumstances, we always have a choice
about our attitude toward the situation.*
Vonette Bright

Considering the Possibilities

*Give your burdens to the LORD,
and he will take care of you.
He will not permit the godly to slip and fall.*
Psalm 55:22 NLT

The Bible teaches us that we need never carry our burdens alone. God is always there, always available, always willing to give us protection, comfort, and support . . . if we'll let Him. Yet sometimes we may find it difficult to hand over our burdens. Why? Because we are imperfect mortals who possess imperfect faith—and because of our doubts, we may be slow to trust even our heavenly Father with the things most important to us. But He is trustworthy, He's all-powerful, and He always has our best interests at heart.

Next time you face a difficult situation or a tough decision, give your burdens to God. He has promised to carry them, and He will keep that promise. Your job is to let go and to give your troubles to the Father. God can bear any burden and tackle any trouble. No problem is too big for Him, Mom, including yours.

Let God's promises shine on your problems.

Corrie ten Boom

The Balancing Act

*Take My yoke upon you and learn from Me, for I am
gentle and lowly in heart, and you will find rest for
your souls. For My yoke is easy and My burden is light.*
Matthew 11:29–30 NKJV

Every mother's life is a delicate balancing act (a
tightrope walk with overcommitment on one
side and undercommitment on the other). And it's
up to you to walk carefully on that rope, not falling
prey to pride (which causes us to attempt too much)
or to fear (which causes us to attempt too little).

God's Word promises us the possibility of
abundance (see John 10:10). And we are far more
likely to experience that abundance when we lead
balanced lives.

Are you doing too much—or too little? If so, it's
time to have a little chat with God. Listen carefully
to His instructions and strive to achieve a more
balanced life, a life that's right for you and your loved
ones. When you do, everybody wins.

*Every one of us is supposed to be a powerhouse for God,
living in balance and harmony within and without.*
Joyce Meyer

When Grief Visits

God, who comforts the downcast, comforted us.
2 Corinthians 7:6 NIV

Grief visits all of us who live long and love deeply. When we lose a loved one, or when we experience any other profound loss, darkness overwhelms us for a while, and it seems as if we cannot summon the strength to face another day—but, with God's help, we can.

Thankfully, God promises that He is "close to the brokenhearted" (Psalm 34:18 NIV). In times of intense sadness, we can turn to Him. When we do, we will be comforted . . . and in time we will be healed.

Holocaust survivor Corrie ten Boom noted, "There is no pit so deep that God's love is not deeper still." Let us remember those words and live by them . . . especially when the days seem dark.

The grace of God runs downhill toward the ones
who are emptied and vulnerable,
toward the ones who admit that they struggle.
Angela Thomas

Happiness and Holiness

Obey God and be at peace with him;
this is the way to happiness.
Job 22:21 NCV

It's an inevitable fact of life, Mom: because you are an imperfect human being, you are not "perfectly" happy—and that's perfectly OK. God is far less concerned with your happiness than He is with your holiness.

God continuously reveals Himself in everyday life, but He does not do so in order to make us contented; He does so in order to draw us to Him. So don't be overly concerned with your current level of happiness: it will change with the phases of your life. Be more concerned with the current state of your relationship with the Creator: He never changes. And because your heavenly Father transcends time and space, you can be comforted in the knowledge that in the end, His joy will become your joy . . . for all eternity.

Happiness is inward and not outward;
and so it does not depend on what we have,
but on what we are.
Henry Van Dyke

Working with Enthusiasm

Do your work with enthusiasm.
Work as if you were serving the Lord,
not as if you were serving only men and women.
Ephesians 6:7 NCV

Are you enthusiastic about life, or do you struggle through each day, giving scarcely a thought to God's blessings? If you're really enthusiastic, consider yourself wise and blessed. But if you're not exactly thrilled about your life, your work, or your future, try focusing on your blessings, not your burdens.

Here's a tip, Mom, for you and your loved ones: don't wait for excitement to find you; find the excitement in life! If you look carefully (and prayerfully), you won't have to search hard to find things worth getting excited about. You'll quickly see that you and your family have more opportunities—and more blessings—than you can count.

Your life is a grand adventure, and your work is profoundly important; so what are you waiting for? Get excited, and get started!

Be enthusiastic.
Every occasion is an opportunity to do good.
Russell Conwell

God's Christmas Gift

There is born to you this day in the city of David a Savior,
who is Christ the Lord. And this will be the sign to you:
You will find a Babe wrapped
in swaddling cloths, lying in a manger.
Luke 2:11–12 NKJV

The familiar words from the second chapter of Luke remind us that the ultimate Christmas gift was presented to mankind in the form of a baby, wrapped in simple clothes, laid in a manger.

The Christ Child was born in the most humble of circumstances: in a nondescript village, to parents of simple means, far from the seats of earthly power. Jesus came not as a conquering king but as a suffering servant. He did not preach a message of retribution or revenge; He spoke words of compassion and forgiveness. We should do our best to imitate Him.

Luke told of shepherds who were tending their flocks on the night Christ was born. May we, like those shepherds of old, leave our fields—wherever they may be—and pause to worship God's priceless gift: His only begotten Son.

The miracle of Christmas is not on 34th Street;
it's in Bethlehem.
Rick Warren

When It's Hard to Be Cheerful

Be cheerful. Keep things in good repair.
Keep your spirits up. Think in harmony. Be agreeable.
Do all that, and the God of love
and peace will be with you for sure.
2 Corinthians 13:11 MSG

On some days, as every mother knows, it's hard to be cheerful. Sometimes, as the demands of the world soar and your energy sags, you may feel less like cheering up and more like tearing up. But even on your toughest days, you can still discover pockets of cheerfulness if you look for them.

If you're taking yourself or your problems too seriously, it's time for an attitude adjustment. So lighten up and chuckle at the occasional absurdities of life. Keep your eye out for people, things, or even just thoughts that can cheer you up. And make it a practice to count your blessings, not your misfortunes. When you do, you'll discover that sometimes happiness comes only when we actively look for it.

We may run, walk, stumble, drive, or fly,
but let us never lose sight of the reason for the journey,
or miss a chance to see a rainbow on the way.
Gloria Gaither

Cooperation

Work at getting along with each other and with God.
Otherwise you'll never get so much as a glimpse of God.
Hebrews 12:14 MSG

Have you and your family members learned the fine art of cooperation? If so, you have gained the wisdom of give-and-take and the foolishness of "me first." Cooperation is the art of compromising on many little things while keeping your eye on one big thing: your family.

But here's a word of warning. If you're like most folks, you're probably a little bit headstrong. You probably want most things done your way—after all, isn't that the best way? Well, if you're observant, you've noticed that people who always insist on "my way or the highway" usually end up with "the highway."

A better way for all concerned (including you) is to abandon the search for "my way" and to search instead for "our way." The happiest families are those in which everybody learns how to give and take . . . with the emphasis on giving.

Cooperation is a two-way street,
but for far too many families, it's the road less traveled.
Marie T. Freeman

Cheerful Generosity

Let each one give as he purposes in his heart,
not grudgingly or of necessity;
for God loves a cheerful giver.
2 Corinthians 9:7 NKJV

Are you a cheerful giver? If you're a mom who's intent on following God's way, you must be. When you give, God looks not only at the quality of your gift but also at the condition of your heart. If you give generously, joyfully, and without complaint, He is pleased. But if you offer your gifts grudgingly, or if your motivation is selfish, you fail to honor your Creator, even though you've gone through the required motions.

Today, Mom, take God's instructions to heart and make a pledge to yourself and your Creator: vow to be a cheerful, generous, courageous giver. The world needs your help, and you'll love the spiritual rewards that will be yours when you give faithfully, prayerfully . . . and cheerfully.

A cheerful giver does not count the cost of what he gives.
His heart is set on pleasing and cheering him
to whom the gift is given.
Juliana of Norwich

God's Faithfulness

*Because of the LORD's faithful love we do not perish,
for His mercies never end.
They are new every morning; great is Your faithfulness!*
Lamentations 3:22–23 HCSB

God is faithful to us—even when we're not very faithful to Him. God keeps His promises to us even when we stray far from His path. He showers us with countless blessings—blessings we don't even always accept. If we are to experience God's love and His grace, we must choose to accept these things from His hand.

God is with you. Listen prayerfully to the quiet voice of your heavenly Father. Talk with God often; seek His guidance; watch for His working; listen to the wisdom He gives through His Word.

God loves you, Mom, and He loves your family. He wants all of you to enjoy the best He has to offer. You can position yourselves to receive His blessings today by being faithful to Him—and the best time to start is now.

People see God every day; they just don't recognize Him.
Pearl Bailey

Surrounded by Opportunities

Make the most of every opportunity.
Colossians 4:5 NIV

Mom, as you look at the landscape of your life, do you see opportunities, possibilities, and blessings, or do you focus on the more negative scenery? If you've acquired the unfortunate habit of focusing too intently on the negative aspects of life, then your spiritual vision is in need of correction.

Whether you realize it or not, opportunities are whirling around you like stars crossing the night sky: beautiful to observe but too numerous to count. Yet you may be too preoccupied with your preordained tasks to notice those opportunities. That's why, occasionally, it's good to slow down and catch your breath. Turn your thoughts toward the talents God has given you and the opportunities He has placed before you. God is leading you in the direction of those opportunities. Your task is to watch carefully, to pray fervently, and to act accordingly.

Life's ups and downs provide windows of opportunity
to determine your values and goals. Think of using
all obstacles as steppingstones to build the life you want.
Marsha Sinetar

The World's Most Important Job

Her children rise up and call her blessed.
Proverbs 31:28 NKJV

Motherhood, other claims to the contrary, is the world's oldest profession—and its most important. This little book of devotional readings has celebrated the joys and responsibilities of the job.

Chinese writer and inventor Lin Yutang once said, "Of all the rights of women, the greatest is to be a mother." Lin understood that a good mother does more than give birth; she shapes life.

Thanks to you, Mom, for all you've done and for all you continue to do. Because of your love and your sacrifices, you are most certainly leaving your mark on the world—and making a difference for eternity. You are indeed blessed.

I looked on child rearing not only as a work of love and duty but as a profession that was fully as interesting and challenging as any honorable profession in the world and one that demanded the best I could bring to it.
Rose Kennedy

Notes

These pages have been provided
for your personal journaling and meditation.

Notes

Notes

Notes

Notes

Notes

Notes

Notes